PRAISE FOR *ACUTE MISFORTUNE*

"This is a marvellous, propulsive, intelligent read."
—CHRISTOS TSIOLKAS

"The terrible force of the painter's rush to self-destruction is matched all the way by the writer's calm mastery of his story."
—HELEN GARNER

"Fierce and spellbinding" —DAVID MARR

"A sober book about a man who was anything but. A clear-eyed, careful account of a squandered life that is generous and unusual in Jensen's refusal to condemn or opine."
—KATE JENNINGS

"The finished work, a quiet triumph of gentle objectivity, is as damning as any blood-and-thunder sermon by Robert Hughes."
—*THE MONTHLY*

"Jensen has a gimlet eye for telling details and images ... At the age of 25, he has also established himself as a keen and elegant prose stylist." —*THE SYDNEY MORNING HERALD*

"Not often do we meet the biographer as pallbearer ... with the journalist's flair for pithy, telling phrases."
—*AUSTRALIAN BOOK REVIEW*

"It was a Faustian contract ... that would place Jensen into physical, even moral, danger. Cullen's self-destruction is horribly riveting." —*AUSTRALIAN FINANCIAL REVIEW*, Best Books of 2014

"Jensen's writing is taut and precise. This novella-sized book stays with you long after you've read it."
—*THE GUARDIAN*, Best Books of 2014

"Raw and uncompromising" —*THE HERALD SUN*

"The book is riveting and sad. A must-read for art lovers."
—*THE DAILY TELEGRAPH*

"Jensen's achievement is remarkable considering his immersion ... It's a pacy, absorbing read."
—*THE AUSTRALIAN*

"Terrifying and terrific" —THE WHEELER CENTRE, Best Books of 2014

"Beautifully designed, eloquently tragic"
—*THE AGE*, Books of the Year

"One of the year's finest endeavours ... There's a raw and volatile beauty to this part-harrowing, part-inspiring tragedy."
—*NEW DAILY*, Top Ten Books of 2014

"A fascinating look at how the creative urge is so often accompanied by the urge for self-destruction."
—*THE COURIER MAIL*

"Jensen's cool eye and determination to avoid the tortured artist clichés makes [the book] weirdly, impressively compelling."
—*WOMEN'S WEEKLY*

"Told with wit, perception and empathy by a young and gifted writer, Erik Jensen's Acute Misfortune, his first book, is a finely written account of the self-destructive, charismatic Australian painter." —*THE WEEKEND AUSTRALIAN*, Best Books of 2014

"Brave, expressive, funny, pungent, revelatory, and at times very sad." —*SYDNEY REVIEW OF BOOKS*

"Jensen has delivered a lucid portrait of a deeply complicated talent; one of the best nonfiction releases of 2014 to date."
—*BOOKS+PUBLISHING*

"Book of the year." —*THE SUNDAY MAIL*

ACUTE MISFORTUNE

ACUTE MISFORTUNE

BY ERIK JENSEN

THE LIFE AND DEATH OF ADAM CULLEN

Published by Black Inc.,
an imprint of Schwartz Publishing Pty Ltd
Level 1, 221 Drummond Street
Carlton VIC 3053, Australia
enquiries@blackincbooks.com
www.blackincbooks.com

This edition published in 2019

9781760640873 (paperback)
9781922231802 (ebook)

A catalogue record for this book is available from the National Library of Australia

Cover design by Josh Ng and Akiko Chan

Printed in Australia by McPherson's Printing Group.

For Nan, who taught me to write.

I intended this to be a longer book,
but we were interrupted.

"ENDURANCE IS MORE IMPORTANT THAN TRUTH"

ADAM MILLER

PROLOGUE

From: Dale Frank
To: Erik Jensen
13/02/2013
7:55 PM

Dear Erik,

It was a real pleasure speaking with you after the exhibition opening.

Despite a personal desire to, I have hesitated since at getting in touch.

Adam first knocked tentatively on my door in late 1986. He was an art student. Opening the door there was an instant association – we both had dark green hair. Some months later he did confess he deliberately had his hair coloured to meet me. I knew him for 15 years, closely, intimately and psychologically as, as he said, "coach, mentor and blackboard" till 2002. I would clarify by saying my unconditional contribution to the friendship continued till 1999, till the advent of excess drugs, his managerial girlfriend, and advent of his "becoming self-aware" knowledge that he was the next Brett Whiteley, which was all just prior to the Archibald.

I am very nervous about continuing a conversation concerning Adam. I do not know your motive. Are you attempting to make a sad figure something he was not, doing an "Archibald" on his character after his death? Adding to the mythology that is already cliché artistic? The basic fact was he was just one young artist among many.

As I believe your genuine intellectual grasp of art nuances go beyond the cliché, I wonder as to the direction of the intended publication.

I was seduced by your charm, good looks and your truffle-like intelligence that evening. But that is maybe, probably, your modus weapon. So it makes me very apprehensive in that what I may say, regarding Adam, may come from playing into that seduction, rather than a distance, for Adam's sake, that I would like to maintain.

Sincerely,

Dale

PROLOGUE

From: Erik Jensen
To: Dale Frank
14/02/2013
10:15 AM

Dear Dale,

It was lovely meeting you, too. I very much enjoyed our conversation and while I understand your hesitation at getting in touch I am glad you did.

The book I am writing contains, I hope, no myth. It is a story of abused talent and excess pathos. It is an account of a man whose lifetime of bravado exhausted him and alienated those around him, but in whose gentle nature there might be some explanation for this impulse. All journalism involves the Sisyphean task of trying to understand other people and in this I have been dealt a boulder called Adam.

The interviews we did over the last four years of his life were unsparingly frank. They were for once free from vainglory – sad, reflexive, perhaps even honest. I have no interest in writing another man's fictions. If it doesn't sound too trite, I might say I am interested only in getting at truth. Talking to you about Adam seemed like truth, where others might have augmented the same events out of guilt or dishonesty.

Of course, I have never pressured anyone to talk to me and I would never write about conversations unless I was certain they were on the record. These were the terms of my very first meeting with Adam. I assure you I have no modus weapon; most days, I would struggle for a modus operandi.

But I greatly enjoyed speaking to you and would love to continue to do so – whether about Adam or not.

Best wishes,

Erik

From: Erik Jensen
To: Dale Frank
25/02/2013
4:56 PM

Dear Dale,

I hope you are well.

It is a little over a week since we exchanged emails and I wanted to be certain my response has not been lost in your inbox. Or – worse – that it had failed in explaining what I am trying to do with this book on Adam. The basic fact that he was one young artist among many is certainly not something I am trying to escape. Indeed, it is likely the premise I am most trying to explain.

Either way, it was certainly a pleasure to meet you.
All the best,
Erik

From: Dale Frank
To: Erik Jensen
27/02/2013
1:22 AM

Dear Erik,
Yes I got your earlier email last week. I'm sorry I did not reply sooner.

I spent this time thinking about you and about what you said in the email, your "public" (?) explanation of your purpose, the mention of the four years of interviews and Adam's approach to you – "sad, reflexive, perhaps even honest." I could actually picture Adam doing his "full of soul" trip on you. The image of this, and my own recollections of him doing this well learnt personality switch-a-roo on others, on myself, made me laugh – inside anyway. It was something Adam knew how to do, that I remember we joked about. He knew he could never get away with it with me. He presented to people what they wanted.

From the few mentions you have made it is clear from what I knew of Adam that he was letting you in. It is a shame you did not have longer because you would have come to recognise this soul trip, and then got past the soft sensitive pretense as well I suspect.

I do not know much if anything of the last 5 or so years of Adam's working relationships, so I cannot comment on your thought that "others might have augmented the same events out of guilt or dishonesty". I just cannot comprehend how anyone would have guilt or recall with dishonesty, unless they are weaving a more enlightened view of themselves into the picture. But I can't see what is to gain.

And this returns me to your motives.

Discussing his failings, his abuses and abusing, his fears, his bigotry, his aggressive self-destruction, his mellow cyanide, alongside any talent, wasted, in an art environment full of jostling equal talent, all goes to mythologising him, unfairly. In the same way the culture has of mythologising other past art figures or figures of "otherness". It is how our culture accommodates and defines talent so not to actually discuss talent.

It is not of any gain to me to say Adam for 18 years responded to me as both someone who could help his career, introduce him to the right people, and equally also as confessor, a therapist of sorts. I am just too cynical, too truthful, too direct, or maybe just too socially inept for artists to put anything over on me, at least personally. Career wise, business, that is another matter.

So a discussion of Adam will be truthful, nothing spared, but in saying that, I will need to give everything I say to you a second thought, a reconsideration, before it is "on the record" because I don't want to disclose everything he and I discussed in confidence, as some things really should NOT be disclosed. Especially if it only goes to become lurid decoration.

His façade of bravado and uncompromising Ego hid the reality, in just the same way as his sad, responsive façade hid the reality. Both were structurally unsound. It was always someone else in control, in command, pulling the levers. Either Adam in the "third person" so to speak, or another person entirely. He had to give these people what they expected, pay the piper, both privately and in his work. He and I discussed this so often. So many "all nights". So many examples.

It is definitely far too dangerous to consider post psychoanalysis as an approach, and I won't be a contributor to that.

So, it is fairly pointless saying I will not talk to you

about Adam, as that is obviously what I have just done!

I hope I can help you with this in some way, so long as its purpose and path stays somewhere in the parameters I see, not mythologising, not embellishing talent beyond its natural peak, nor creating a tragic figure.

With best wishes,

Dale

From: Erik Jensen
To: Dale Frank
27/02/2013
6:10 PM

Dear Dale,

I'm glad you wrote back. I understand your cautionary advice, and I think I have perhaps failed in conveying the complexity I saw in Adam's character. He had a series of acts – and a major in performance, which is always important to remember – and I think I saw most of them. I think I also saw behind them – the bits where the act ran out, or where a question forced a chink between pretenses.

Anyhow, I suspect this is not your main concern.

I suspect your concern is to wonder why a book might be written about Adam at all: Whether I might be a hatchet man looking to dress up a corpse, or an acolyte looking for stories to embroider a myth. I hope I am neither.

I am not writing about Adam because of his art, although that was obviously why he called me in the first place. I am writing a character study in which art – in the end – is not the most important part. Joseph Mitchell wrote about stevedores and barflies not because his particular subject was the best at lugging grain or drinking scotch; he wrote because the rest of them was interesting, irrespective of that first fact and not because of it.

I understand there is no way to write about a painter without privileging on some level his talent above the many other talents of his generation. But talent is not my subject. Art is not even really my subject. This is not a public explanation and nor was my earlier email. It is simply an honest answer to the question you have raised. I think – if I might be so bold – we are on the same page.

But your emails have helped me to clarify a lot of my thinking. Thank you for that.

I hope we continue communicating.

Best,

Erik

DEATH

"I think the art world caused this."

Coffins weigh more than you expect. Adam's is heavy, although he leaves it mostly empty, his body battered and made small by illness. Behind me, the critic Andrew Frost jokes it is full of gold bars. No one laughs. The comic Mikey Robins strains and weeps silent tears. Neither of them has seen Adam in years. Few in this clutch of pallbearers have.

Adam's is a funeral of friends who have become acquaintances, spurred back into friendship by death. Catharine Lumby, who has written the obituary in the *Sydney Morning Herald* a few days earlier, arrives late and finds a seat beside Robins. A soft-pack of Kleenex rests between them. Charles Waterstreet, the barrister who will give Adam's eulogy, is later still and picks his way through the pews under the cover of a piped hymn – always too tall, and especially now.

Adam's final drug dealer, who sold him the narcotic pain reliever OxyContin from a fibro house on the Great Western Highway, turns up during the second half of the service. He has stringy hair and a stringier girlfriend and is forced to sit with the journalists. This is more than dull symbolism: in the final years of Adam's life, drug dealers and journalists were the figures he saw most. Adam had decided he needed them more than he needed friends.

"Adam Cullen was a damned inconvenient friend," begins Waterstreet, who had won Adam the suspended sentence he never lived to serve. "He died in the middle of the Olympics. Typical."

In his rounded-off diction, Waterstreet pays tribute to the character Adam had hoped to be. He makes generous comparisons to William S. Burroughs and Hunter S. Thompson, the writer-pistolmen who became more important to Adam than other artists, of whose freedom he was acutely jealous and in whose fame he found his own justification. Waterstreet races when he hints at what killed Adam, as if the lawyer in him feels it must be said but that still he would rather not be saying it.

"It was not heroin or drugs that pulsed through his veins, it was turpentine and paint," he says. "He died with paint in his veins and lived his life with a colourful purpose, out loud, proving nothing was as it seems, but underneath it was often the opposite."

He describes the crippling shyness Adam carried since birth and hints at the burden of a success Adam never quite believed he had earned. He makes sense of the inevitability hanging in the room: the fact that Adam was always going to die young.

"Adam was exhausted. His health and the stress of his life, of court, just sucked him dry," Waterstreet says. "You can map his ascent into the heaven of professional life – and descent into the hell of drink, drugs and addiction – and his re-ascent into heaven in his later years: before the Archibald with David Wenham and the smiling, fresh-faced boy wonder he was ... later becoming the swashbuckling huntsman, always a gentleman, that he presented."

The eulogy – even as it is being read – has the title of Waterstreet's weekly *Sun-Herald* column typed at its top.

*

It was Sunday when I called his father, Kevin. The third-last day of July 2012. There was no need to ask the question. I had twice tried Adam's phone, but there was no space for new messages. There never was. "You know, don't you?" Kevin said. "The police are there now. And the ambulance. They're – they're going to take him away."

Kevin started to cry. Tears welled up in his vowels and ended his sentences in muffled yelps. He had been with Adam two days earlier. "He agreed to go into rehab on Monday," he said, struggling to force the words out of his mouth. "We left some money for him."

I agreed to call Adam's friends and tell them he was dead. Kevin dug around for numbers. In the end, there were only three. Adam's life had contracted hugely in the decade since he moved to the Blue Mountains, outside Sydney. His last two relationships had broken down. Friends had drifted away as he became more difficult, as the course of his life became more obvious and its conclusion more inevitable. Adam spent a career creating a character for himself – a wild man, kept alive by capricious talent – but eventually he tired of the role he had spent all that time writing. He no longer had the energy to ape the person he was supposed to be.

"I couldn't really see Adam just disappearing away into ignominy," Kevin said, having put down the phone for a time to compose himself. "We will never know what was in his head. Except his mother will know; Carm will know."

*

St Rose of Lima in Collaroy is a modern church with ceiling fans and a font that looks like a suburban water feature. The walls are blonde brick and the roof is held up by exposed rafters. A wide-eyed rendition of the stations of the cross runs up one wall, like the souvenir from a holiday to Mexico. Posters advertising World Youth Day are stuck to another. Two years ago almost to the day, Adam's mother, Carmel, was mourned here. He attended primary school opposite, with the art dealer Jason Martin, who today would carry his coffin. The Berith Street house in which he grew up is less than a block away, although he had no memory of coming here as a child.

It looks for a while that Adam will not fill the pews, that the folding chairs set to one side will be left empty. But by the time the first hymn tumbles through the church speakers, the room is brimful. It plays in an out-of-reach register to a mouthing congregation. The great round jaw Adam inherited from his mother sings out from the O'Loughlans in the crowd. At the front of the hall is a print of Growler, the dog Adam never tired of mourning. "He died peacefully," forgotten relatives say of Adam, waiting for the sermon, having not seen him for years. "He was a terrible sufferer."

Turning over in my head is a line from an interview Adam gave the *Bulletin* a decade earlier, his definition of art: "It's the only profession in the world where your employer wants you to die." I think, in this strangely griefless church, it is perhaps the most honest description he gave of his career. I count up the art dealers in the room: there are four.

*

In his welcome, Father Michael Hwang reads a series of platitudes to a still tearless crowd. "His life is a canvas that is now finished," he says. "His life was his masterpiece." An odd collection of pictures plays through a projector: a newspaper shot of Adam leaving court after pleading guilty in his weapons case; a painting by him of Mussolini; another work called "Holy Sordid Experience", its clothed terriers dancing beside a child's buggy and the words "God is away on business, he has joined the Mob". There is a photograph of the party held at the Bayswater Brasserie after he won the Archibald Prize and another, published in *Time Out* magazine, of him brandishing a revolver, wearing like a toupee the echidna carcass he has pulled from a tanning bath.

His second cousin, the actor Max Cullen, reads from the book of Ecclesiastes, cat-faced and dishevelled, looking slept-in and surprised as he always does. He is wearing a tie on an open-necked shirt and a pair of glasses on a length of cord. Leaving the pulpit, he waits two beats, as if for an unseen dramaturge. He turns on his mark, running back with one finger extended: "The word of the Lord."

It becomes clear just how important the Archibald Prize was to Adam. It is mentioned in the priest's welcome, the homily, the eulogy. The Archibald was how Adam made friends, particularly as he distanced himself from the world. Many of his subjects are here: Robins, Waterstreet, David Wenham, Max. Nelson Woss, who sat for Adam's final Archibald portrait with the kelpie from his film *Red Dog*, is among the mourners who will repair to Una's schnitzel house in Darlinghurst for slabs of meat and oversized beers after the wake. The painter Gareth Sansom, who sat for Adam in 2010, will attend a smaller gathering on top of the Cullen, the Melbourne hotel founded on Adam's name and a collection of his art.

Outside the church, his father seems impatient with the holy water. "Cop this," he says, flinging the aspergillum at the coffin. "Cop this, mate." Mourners start to build up near the hearse. Kevin takes my shoulders in his hands and tells me to wet the coffin. "Have a sprinkle," he says. "Wash him clean."

The hearse draws slowly up the drive, followed by Kevin. These final unrehearsed moments have the precision of a military ceremony. Nothing is said. Press flashbulbs explode as the car turns into an empty street. Adam's body disappears wordlessly into the suburbia of his childhood. Kevin stands at the gates. He reaches across to hold the hand of his new partner, a man now profoundly alone.

*

At the wake, in a hall behind the church, old women offer cans of Guinness and tepid cocktail frankfurts with tomato sauce. By chance, students from the neighbouring primary school have been studying Adam in art class. Their wonkily painted Ned Kellys are pinned down one wall, a final rejoinder to the long-prosecuted charge that children could do what Adam did.

The wake is a conversation of two questions, played out in small circles, tinged with gentle shame: "When did you last see Adam?" and "Do you know how he died?" The first is answered mainly in years, the latter with silent looks. "The paper said he died in bed," says one cousin. "So, does that mean an overdose?"

In the end, Adam did not need to overdose. Drugs had been working quietly on his body for two decades. At times, more loudly. He was weakened by narcotics and made wretched by drink. His organs were ravaged. He could no longer eat solids. In his bathroom, he kept a collection of hospital bracelets hanging from his mirror, like an adult's baby book, each discharge a strange kind of rebirth. He did not need to overdose; he was already dead.

*

A few days before the funeral, Ian Howard, an important early teacher, posted a message on an online memorial. It was in Howard's New Art Forms course that Adam had produced the work which would most define him as a young artist: a performance in which he chained a pig's head to his ankle and dragged it around until it began to disintegrate and his fellow art students began to revile him. It was this creation of distance and revulsion that formed his worldview. He felt bitterly that he had been rejected, all the while making work that asked people to reject him.

"Adam respectfully kept in touch – sometimes through generosity, sometimes through need," Howard wrote. "In a deliberately supporting statement to the magistrate who was hearing his drunk driving and possession of guns charge, I wrote: 'Adam Cullen has been a "risk taker" in his image making for decades. From the successes, his contribution and reputation stems. Never has this risk taking been reckless of his own or anyone else's safety or wellbeing. Adam often tests himself but never others, except in the sense of an audience being the willing observers of a confronting work of art.' Of course I lied about Adam never being reckless about his own safety and wellbeing. It seemed the right thing to say at the time ... perhaps now, it was not."

A week later, Adam was the last item in the parish newsletter. A man thoroughly eulogised was, finally, a series of bland acknowledgements. He talked a lot about "aesthetic residue", about what he would leave behind. His last marks were not ones of sadness, however, but mild inconvenience:

> Last Friday we said farewell to Adam Cullen, Kevin & Carmel's son. A big thank you to Josie Vescio and the St Rose school community for making their hall and grounds available for Adam's wake, to the parishioners and office staff who provided the food and drink for the wake and to Year 6 from Wheeler Heights School for the artwork tribute to Adam they set up in the hall.

*

The first time I met Adam, he told me he was going to die. That was four years ago. He was forty-two. "I know that I will be dead," he said, "because I'm so busy dying."

We were standing in his bedroom, beside a sheetless mattress. Down from a burst pillow floated just above the floor. From the door you could make out a stack of dishes ossifying in the kitchen. Death was mentioned without drama. Nor was it said in sadness. He was answering, unprompted, the questions of his own racing logic. "I would never kill myself," he said, although the question was never asked. "I'm not fucking gutless. I get depressed, but I'm not fucking gutless."

The bed had a wet smell, like rain had got into a dusty room. It was piled with curios: animal skins and merchandise from shooting clubs. A Templar helmet sat where the pillows should have been, memento of a trip to Spain.

"Everything moves towards its end," Adam said. "As soon as you're born, you're busy dying. And I am dying. I suppose I've just been smashing my head against the wall of existence for just a little bit too long."

We spent a few hours that day in Adam's glass-fronted studio, overhanging the Grose Valley, on the edge of Wentworth Falls. He paid a landlady in paintings for the smallish room that looked out at dark bushland and the glinting suburbs of the city's approaches.

For me, the studio came to symbolise his mind. On one wall was the private in Adam's life: a missive he claimed a girlfriend had written for him when he came out of hospital, sketched in what was unmistakably his hand. "I can do this," it read. "I have no fear. I am a great painter." On the other wall, the part of him society saw: an assured signature, painted in block letters on an otherwise blank canvas. These were the two parts of his anxiety – the tension that had become his life – above which a pink swastika was sprayed on the ceiling. The room was almost always empty, nervous with spilt paint, stacked occasionally with canvases. And when he stood there, which he did almost every night, there was nowhere to hide from the world as it rushed in through the glass.

To prove on this first meeting the conviction he felt about his own death, Adam unbuttoned his shirt to show me a scar that twisted the length of his torso. His stomach looked like an overstuffed carpetbag, stitched poorly at the fastenings. He forced his thumbs into drain holes on either side of his abdomen – ports from the operation that a year earlier had removed his gallbladder and much of his pancreas, and which had healed as enormous pockmarks burred by infection. I asked him what had happened, to fill the silence more than anything. "Acute misfortune," he said. "I think the art world caused this."

PERSONA

"Everything is on the record. Everything else is fucking gutless."

It is by accident that Adam shoots me. We are camped on a bend of the Turon River, past Hill End, in the sheep-paddocked middle of New South Wales. Adam and I have been drinking vodka all day, him toasting each mugful: "*Arriba el culo*; up your bum, no babies."

A dead kangaroo is hanging from a tree, shot with a revolver as we pulled up the night before. Adam had fired a few rounds into the campsite darkness, and it was only in the morning that we found the carcass where it had struggled to climb an embankment. I had spent the evening hiding in the car, worried by the handful of ammunition Adam had thrown into the fire he was sitting beside. By the afternoon we are both drunk, and I am too close when Adam fires off a round of birdshot. The spray catches me in the thigh.

It hurts less than expected. I am wearing heavy jeans, my legs numb with cold and drink. I taste metal in my mouth and then a kind of sweet wooziness. My tongue is dry from liquor. In the end there are only a few pellets, high up and glancing. I will dig them out with a pair of tweezers at home the following evening, sitting on the lid of my toilet. "Terribly fucking sorry, mate," Adam says. "Terribly fucking sorry."

It is an accident, but also a kind of test. Adam is never satisfied until he knows where the boundaries are, until he knows how far he can push a person. "I have heard this a few times from people," he says. "'I can't spend too much time with you, Adam. You're too dangerous.' I do take things a bit far, but it's not with other people. It's with myself."

Adam's reflections on himself are always reflections on purpose. How one should live is a favourite topic. The advice has been harvested from Schopenhauer and Nietzsche, and is delivered with bitterness that the world is not more the way he wants it to be. "I thought we were here to wear ourselves out. Isn't that the trip?" he says. "I'd hate to be really old and just boring. People are too judgemental because they're scared cunts. I think – or I thought – I was sort of helping."

Later, Adam throws me from the back of a motorcycle. It is not an accident. He reaches back and pushes me off in one smooth motion, just before we take the hairpin bend that holds his house in place on the edge of Wilson Park. Cold air stings against my grazes, and the back tire tears up my shirt in the fall. There is white pain in my wrist and gravel buried in my hand, but nothing is broken.

He doubles back and stops beside me. Reaching down with one arm, his legs still straddling the motorcycle, he offers to help me up. He smiles a little as I take his hand: "How was that?"

*

Adam viewed art as a means of checking whether society was still paying attention. He always wanted to see how far a person would go, how willing they were to join him. In a strange way, he wanted to know if they could keep up. "I think that sacrifice is everything," he said. "You sort of have to sacrifice yourself. You have to stick your neck out – this whole thing of endurance."

He was preparing to deliver his favourite quote: a line of Bukowski's, never attributed, that Adam wrote in the front of all his books and offered as explanation for most of his acts. He inscribed gifts with it, and the words would end up on a memorial card printed after he died. His father did not realise the words were not Adam's. In a sentence, it said everything he thought about life: "Endurance is more important than truth."

The line was from the film *Barfly*, a loosely autobiographical fairytale of drunken talent, ambiguous as to whether the brilliance of Mickey Rourke's character has been squandered on scotch and waters, or whether he needs them to write. The film was a checklist of Adam's beliefs: that art could not be made in comfort, that drinking was to be revered, that there was beauty to be found in squalor.

Adam saw the film in 1987, when it was first released, although it would be another twenty years before he read Bukowski, just as his first symptoms of alcohol-related pancreatitis were showing. That was how Adam absorbed culture: in fragments. He spent his life a scavenger. "Anybody can be a non-drunk," Rourke's character says as he accepts a cheque for his first published work. "It takes a special talent to be a drunk. It takes endurance. Endurance is more important than truth."

Adam continued instead: "I don't know what truth is. It's such an abstract term, truth. Truth is active, but people are scaredy-cats. They want something to rely on, but there's nothing there."

*

People loved Adam. It was his voice they remembered most, then his eyes. They were his mother's: dancing, intense, never quite settling as one colour or another. "I don't know what colour Adam's eyes are," his father said. "They're all mixed up, like something in the bottom of one of his damn paint tins." Adam stole girls with them when he was at art school. They could fix people in place if he wanted them to, a talent he exploited early in his career. "I used to be quite handsome," he said by way of explanation. "A little blond boy and quite fucking handsome."

The voice came from somewhere calmer than Adam ever was. It was helped along with cigarettes, although it never lost its mellifluousness. It was a radio voice and it gave assurance to everything he said. Adam used it to great effect. It was the only constant in a charisma on which he built a career and ran out two lifetimes' worth of friendships. It was the ballast for his restlessness.

As with the colour of his eyes, Adam's signature never settled. With each year it lost another letter, until it was a single loping A, tailed by a rush of peaks and troughs – like a lie feeding out of a polygraph machine. "I just wanted it to be this mark," Adam said: "Up, down and around and around. With time it will lose those marks, too. I always had a terrible signature."

*

Adam's first significant mention in the press was incidental: a positive reference deep down in a review of several shows, written by the curator Felicity Fenner for the arts pages of the *Sydney Morning Herald*. It was May 1993 and the sculptor Hany Armanious had included an installation of Adam's in the seminal grunge show *Shirthead*. The show – the last at Mori Annexe before it closed – was described as a final childhood romp for the artists involved. Adam exhibited a teddy bear sprinkled with naphthalene flakes, the lining of a chocolate box upturned on its head like a helmet. Already, the major themes of his career were showing. Fenner called it "a poignant mixture of childhood innocence and adult malevolence". While the mention was incidental, it was also prophetic: Hany and Adam, Fenner wrote, "represent the cool end of the grunge movement and are two of the most interesting artists here".

Six months passed before Adam was made the subject of a feature, again in the *Sydney Morning Herald.* It was the newspaper Adam most often read and to which he most owed his career. In the piece, Catharine Lumby held him up as a new kind of artist produced by the recession of the early 1990s. A photograph of him in his Annandale studio was taken to accompany the story.

From here, he became a fixture in the press. His shows were almost always reviewed. In print, you could track writers as they turned to his work. The language often went from dismissive to hesitantly reverential. His art was discussed on the letters pages of newspapers. When journalists called, he was always good for a quote.

"Cullen's works traffic in a suburban readymade aesthetic – a recent work, for instance, consisted of a stuffed cat, lovingly wrapped and bandaged like an accident victim. It's innovative and exciting, but hardly what the average commercial buyer is likely to put in their boardroom," wrote Lumby, whose sister Adam started seeing around this time. "Like many artists of his generation, however, Cullen has no expectation of making money from his practice. 'It's a non-issue,' he says. 'Totally irrelevant.'"

*

The fruit trees in Adam's garden never set their crops. There is an apple and two apricots, their arms gnarled and slightly twisted, stunted by a driveway and the large drinks fridge Adam says he will fill with sculpture if he is ever selected for the Venice Biennale. He says the garden is a hanging swamp, but in truth it is just overgrown. The trees look as if they've been abused. They cower in front of the house. A trailer full of bush rock shuts in the Holden FC that Adam would drive if a court had not taken his licence. A sign on the front door reads "Beware of the God".

It takes a while to get the lights on and we are in the back room by the time Adam finds a seat. This is the house the Archibald bought but did not pay off, where he was supposed to settle down with Carrie Lumby. There is a couch spread along one wall, looking to a television and a coffee table crowded with cigarette butts and insulin needles. Adam won the Woollahra Small Sculpture Prize in 2008 for gluing the table's contents to a jamón stand and spray-painting it silver.

The back room is connected to the rest of the house by an unused kitchen. On the edge of this precipice, a table is piled with unopened mail: overdue notices on his mortgage, invitations to art shows, unpaid ambulance bills. There is a bathroom off to one side, not much more than a shower and a toilet, the floor lined with wet towels that have dried to fit around the vanity. In the front is a dark room where Adam hoards taxidermy. Two bedrooms come off it, although he sleeps mostly on the couch.

Adam puts his hands into his pockets and removes three billiard balls stolen from the pub we have just left.

He pulls a Dremel engraver from under the couch and starts cutting his initials into the balls, a block-lettered answer to his loping signature. Adam signed everything. Occasionally, he spoke in the third person. He was proud that his name meant something.

"I'll always be a sort of existentialist, an aesthetic Catholic," he says, settling in for one of his dissertations on the Irish. "Let's face it: Jesus Christ was crucified by the English in Northern Ireland." Adam is turning the billiard balls over in his hands. Alcohol has dulled his senses and his Dremel cannot get purchase on the rounded surfaces. "I'm more Irish than the bloody Irish," he says. "I could walk anywhere on Bell's Road. That's bloody Irish."

Adam has never been to Ireland.

*

The phrase *enfant terrible* attaches itself and never leaves. Adam dresses for it, in elaborate boots and outsized hats. An adolescent talent for shock has become an adult hallmark. There is – mostly, at least – enough wit to take off the edge. Adam says of the director Neil Armfield, whom he was commissioned to paint for the National Portrait Gallery, that he "had a smile like a little boy who's pissed himself and knows it's funny". The same is true of him.

Interviews with Adam follow a predictable arc. He surprises one journalist by producing a screed of paper from which he reads a list of thoughts he feels are important to the piece. In his final years he becomes something of a bored tour guide, showing people through his life.

Invariably, Adam begins these later interviews by claiming his girlfriend has just left him. It makes writers forgiving of his anger, and explains away the mess that is his house. His next trick is to take the journalist to his studio, usually before they have been inside. The change of location is disorienting, he tells me, and it puts him in charge. Adam barks the same command as the photographer's car turns down the steep driveway leading to the studio, and it is printed in at least one profile: "Keep right. Keep right. A few friends have lost cars down there."

As if on cue, he points out a stone wall beside his studio and claims it was built by Sidney Nolan. The grand white house behind his work space was once the Boyds', he tells everyone. If he likes the journalist, he ends the interview by digging around in a pile of books and paper and giving them an etching. It is an act of calculated generosity, a gift that makes the journalist feel they are somehow special, that this famously difficult man has decided to let them in. Mine is the scratchy outline of a child's face. It is called "Infant".

"I've always painted human beings in various stages of physical and psychological trauma," he tells Joyce Morgan in one profile. "I am drawn to people by their psychological intensity. I don't care if it's an actor or ex-con or a plumber or some crazed gun freak. Or that guy." Adam is priming himself, preparing to borrow Bon Scott for a point he has made a hundred times before. "He's so ugly but so sexy. I like people with a death wish."

And it works. Morgan is impressed. She writes of a technique Adam has spent two decades perfecting: "He peppers his conversation with such provocative, declarative statements. Comments delivered apparently off-the-cuff but crafted with an attention to detail. 'Now these quotes are very easy to fuck up because they could be twisted if you miss out a conjunction,' he warns."

*

Adam was in his late twenties when he told Carrie that he had a brother who had died from a heroin overdose. By this time he was using heroin himself. He said the brother had been a surfer, an outgoing boy who spent long, perfect hours at the beach with his father and found easy success with women.

Caricature fascinated Adam. As a teenager, he drew cartoons for the local paper. He had a handful of personas he used for different occasions: sometimes he was the sensitive artist, misunderstood by a cruel world; more often he was the dangerous provocateur, dispatching paintings from the fringes of life so that the rest of society would not have to live there. The smaller he became – the angrier, the more cut off – the larger the characters got. His friendship with the standover man Mark "Chopper" Read, whom he met in 2002, intensified the act. Both were performers and they learnt from each other. "I suppose I put things on a bit," Adam told me. "I'm not always happy with who I am."

It was not until Carrie brought up Adam's dead sibling at a family occasion that he admitted the story was an invention: a description of the boy Adam wished he had been, a version of the father he idolised, cut down by the drug that had become his addiction. He did have a half-brother, Mark, who outlived him.

*

The last serious profile of Adam was written for *Good Weekend* during one of his bouts of pancreatitis. It appeared in late November 2008, under the title "The Devil in Adam Cullen". All the predictable tropes were there: the just-departed girlfriend, the dramatic mention of his diabetes, the trip to the studio. Adam started the interview as he always did: late. He began in a flannel dressing gown and a tiger-fur belt, and ended it with a severed goat's head on his lap, a hunting trophy he had pulled from the freezer. "Cullen grasps a rusty trumpet off a nearby shelf and starts playing, badly, *The Last Post*," Janet Hawley wrote. "It is clearly time to go."

And yet, as always with Adam, time was made for dictation: "I paint human car crashes. I'm not a romantic painter; I'm the inverse, I romance the dark side of life. I'm not afraid to explore it. Most people are too scared to look at the dark side, too fearful to face their own demons – so they don't explore it and don't understand it. Everyone loves a car crash, but they stare from a safe distance. I go right up close."

Hawley got all three acts of the Adam Cullen Show: the provocative showman, the dark intellectual and, finally, the repentant Catholic. "Next morning, Cullen phones, gentle as a lamb," she reported. "'I'm trying to get rid of that bad boy image,' he says, and asks me not to mention several other things from the previous day. 'I'm 43 now, a more mature and reflective person. I might say things that sound outrageous – but they're actually not. We need to talk some more.'"

*

It is early 2008, a month after Adam and I first meet, when I get my phone call. I had interviewed him for a profile in the *Sydney Morning Herald* and he had enjoyed the piece. He asks if I will write his biography. "Thames & Hudson want it," he says. "And I'd like you to write it, digger."

Within a week, I am staying in Adam's spare room. I am nineteen and impulsive. It is Adam's studied disobedience that draws me to him, his mischief. I am intrigued by his reputation and disbelieving of his stories. Over the next few days, we begin a series of conversations that will last four years. They begin as manifesto: observations about himself, polished over two decades, that approximate in varying degree his several personas. For the first six months at least, they are stitched with lies. With time, they become more honest.

"People don't like you to change. People like to have you as one thing," Adam says in this first week. "They like reliable. They like a harmless, good-looking, reliable failure. Sorry, I'm not that. I used to be good-looking, but I'm not reliable. I don't care about people."

He begins a riff on notoriety. Modesty is not a mark of our early conversations. "It's not a conscious thing. Everything I do: I can't help if people like it or they don't. It isn't my fault everyone else is so fucking boring."

I never hear from Thames & Hudson and I begin to doubt the deal existed.

ART

"I love it because it's so useless."

The day Adam's retrospective closes at the Art Gallery of New South Wales, he stands in his garden wearing only his underpants and he cries. It is the end of July 2008. Through the tears, he yells into the morning, willing that the show be kept open in perpetuity, that it become a memorial. He yells and cries and yells for half an hour and then he goes inside. Sitting on his couch, in front of a vase of dead cornflowers, he fires a sawn-off shotgun into the ceiling above him.

"I was crying," he says on the phone, immediately afterwards. "That's not Adam Cullen. It's the last day of my show and I just need to call someone. I'm really upset. I think it should be there forever."

This is during a brief dry period. The drugs have not stopped, but the alcohol has. "I have been like fucking Thor since I haven't had a drink. I can clap thunder out of every brush. I can't talk enough."

He says he views his job as ministering to a kind of national hospice. When Adam speaks, he has a jumbled lucidity. He spends so much time alone, rolling phrases over in his mind, that when he comes to voice them they are often badly contorted. He frequently calls his work palliative care, a means of making the world more comfortable while it perishes around him. "There's a big part of Australia that's actually dead," he says.

A week later, he is drunk.

*

Paint was Adam's first memory. He remembered as a toddler tipping an open tin of enamel over himself. His cloth nappy drank in the blue paint until it was wet through and he was finally found in the mess by his mother, who cleaned him up but did not scold him. He could remember the weight of the tin just before he knocked it over, and the coolness of the paint as it poured out across him. "I don't know what it means," he said. "But it's the first thing I can remember."

Adam failed his painting subjects at the City Art Institute, under the tutelage of Sydney Ball, yet painting remained the talent he could not escape. He avoided it for a long time, having shown aptitude as a child. Eventually, he could not deny its pull. "He was a old cunt even then," Adam said of Ball. "I mean, what the fuck is 'Paint Technology'?"

Adam was a painter of many subjects – of hurt and longing, occasionally even of machismo – but fundamentally he was a painter of muscle. It was with both pride and curiosity that he skinned the animals he killed while hunting, and his paintings had the same subcutaneous impulses. This explains the black lines that became a signature in his later acrylic pictures: he would begin each painting as a mess of muscle and sinew, the subject a confusion of colours, imperceptible until it was finally described by the lines of eloquent black laid down on top of it. His skill came more from the cartoons he drew in his teens than it did from study. The tricks were all cartooning shorthands.

But the paintings, when they were good, were pointedly sophisticated. The muscle he started with went some way to guaranteeing this. They were paintings of anxiety painted from anxiety. They were made always in the late evening, following an afternoon of agitation. Adam was disciplined about his work: his schedule fixed him in the studio from eight pm until after midnight. His days would be spent mostly in sleep. "There's just more to paint about at night. I can't make any excuses. It's just me and it, only me and it," he said. "It's all in my head. I just have to pick out these individual signifiers in this vast landscape before me."

He talked about "executing" paintings. It took him a long time to build up to them, to worry himself into a state of panic and keep worrying until his disquiet was finally hurried onto the canvas. He viewed the act almost as performance art. "They're not paintings," he said. "They are a recording, the final document."

*

In the early 1990s Adam was placed among a group of artists making what was called "Avant Grunge" – a movement with which no one identified, invented by Jeff Gibson in an essay of the same name. Adam made a habit at the time of living above pharmacies, and was living above one on King Street in Newtown with Hany Armanious, another proponent of the phantom school.

Despite their proximity, they did not bond. Adam was always working odd jobs: he had the ethic of a builder's son and this, at least in his telling, was what prevented him from fitting in with other artists. In Hany's recollection, Adam was unemployed and Hany was working as a landscape gardener. "I was fucking working in a funeral parlour on bucket duty," Adam said. "We'd go in and mop the person up when all that was left was juices. Hany was on the dole and showered twice a day."

Adam was mostly a sculptor at this point. He made scrappy works from used pens and unfired clay, giving them long names hewn from theory and nonsense. Everything looked as if it had been broken and he had tried clumsily to fix it. These signs of caring were the works' charm, and they were lost to some end in his paintings – perhaps because painting came more easily. The sculptures grew out of performances at art school: the lawnmower he started on stage; the cat he skinned while the Doors played; the cassettes he stitched to the soles of his feet; the pig's head ball and chain that sparked his notoriety.

His sculptural masterwork, *Residual paroxysm of unspoken and extended closures interrogated by a malady of necrogenic subterfuge with a nice exit,* finally sold to the Art Gallery of New South Wales in 2008, almost two decades after being shown there as a part of the era-defining Perspecta shows. It was, like many of his assemblages, maternal. An air-conditioning unit, padded with disposable nappies, sits in a bathtub, connected to a television by a length of plastic tubing and, further on, to a battery of pharmaceutical instruments and drying mucus. The impression is of a failed life support, an ectopic womb. The unplugged television exists as an aborted power source. It is an extension of the idea explored in *Cosmological satellite mother denied depressed speech,* a beer keg to which he affixed a length of umbilical cord preserved in formalin, a specimen stolen from a closed teaching hospital. The works represented what had nurtured Adam: television, and then beer.

"It's taken me eighteen years to fucking sell it," he said by way of celebration. "They take this fucking shit out of my house and call it art. It's just so great."

*

Adam never started on the doctorate he talked about in his final years: *Death in Australian Art.* He bought a monograph on Sidney Nolan but got no further. Perhaps fittingly, he died before he began.

A decade earlier, at the University of New South Wales' College of Fine Arts, Adam had completed a master's thesis he called *Birth of an Idiot – or Where I Would Have Got if I'd Been Stupid.* His model was the Jerilderie Letter, Ned Kelly's 8000-word manifesto, dictated to Joe Byrne in the summer of 1879. Adam treasured his edition of the letter. He marked his place in it with a notice from his own probation officer, as if he and Kelly were both outlaws conversing across the centuries. "This is Ned Kelly's DNA," he said when he lent it to me. "It's his bloody DNA on the page." I was at home before I realised the line was Peter Carey's, and it was printed on the book's cover.

Adam said he wrote *Birth of an Idiot* in a single afternoon with the assistance of a six-pack of beer. This was not true. The thesis began as a map of the "psychic geography of the Australian landscape". Esoteric language aside, it was an attempt by Adam to characterise his portraiture as a kind of suburban landscape painting. Certainly, he never tried to escape the flatness of Australia. He made paintings of the vast spaces between things. Faces became mountains; his lurid backgrounds, the sky. Text was now the horizon line. Some of this was wit: "Art has to look like art. Children grow up to be just like adults." Some of it was openly mocking of academia: in his footnotes Adam quoted the jingle of a Pizza Hut commercial, and noted Pro Hart's contribution to the Stainmaster brand of carpets.

"I make no attempt to frame my investigations in traditional methodological terms. Like my practice itself, this text is not so readily classifiable; its meanings remain ambiguous and incomplete. Instead, what emerges from this piece of writing is a kind of self-critical story," he wrote in the abstract. "So, instead of being a generalised theoretical account, this has become a neurotic chronicle, composed by a corpulent stooge … The opinions expressed in this story aren't necessarily shared by the rest of the world. Nor should they be. As Mike Kelley says: 'Too much is always expected of love and art.'"

The thesis acknowledged Adam's experiences of intoxication and isolation, although it did not press these themes. It recounted fondly the television of his childhood: *Lancelot Link, Secret Chimp*; *Phantom Agents*; *Captain Scarlet*; *Thunderbirds*. "TV has always been there for me," he wrote. "As a child, I would eat, sleep and get ready for school in front of television. It was my way of getting out of the house. It taught me to see and to use my imagination."

Birth of an Idiot praised the suburbs as the apex of human development, a site of endless nourishment undeserving of cynicism. But at the heart of the essay was a desire to engage with the bush of his parents' youth – a longing, as he would later express it, to live their country childhoods.

This same longing had given rise to the most indelible image of Adam's youth, a provocation that fascinated him and from which he never recovered:

> I was an adolescent, and like most white, middle-class, male teenagers from the northern beaches of

> Sydney, I hadn't experienced anything. It was in the far west of NSW on a sheep property. I was in the company of two older cousins and two dogs. We were in a truck pig-shooting in the blackness of early morning in God's Own Country. My cousins caught a large red kangaroo by lassoing it on the run. While two kelpie bitches held it down, they proceeded to cut its tail off with a chainsaw. At the time I thought it was pretty amusing, it certainly held my attention.

There was morose comedy in the kangaroo, Samson-like, its strength gone as it tried hopelessly to right itself without a tail. Adam brought this up occasionally. Sometimes he laughed; sometimes, it caused him to cry. He felt a need to match the attention-grabbing nature of this act, and at the same time live up to its masculinity.

The closest thing he had to a model was the German artist Martin Kippenberger, who died while Adam was writing his thesis – suffering a "ferocious liver", as Adam quaintly put it. "Playfully vicious and hopelessly addicted to self-parody," he wrote. "Kippenberger reconstructs normalcy and makes it hysterically tragic."

The final line of *Birth of an Idiot* quoted Martin Bryant, who had killed thirty-five people and wounded twenty-three more at Port Arthur two years earlier. This was a man said to buy round-the-world plane tickets so that he might talk to the person in the seat beside him, whose parents chained him up because they could not contain his energy. "I wanted to meet up with normal people," Bryant said, "but it didn't work."

*

Adam was a painter by the time he started the thesis in 1997, but only just. He had exhibited a collection of pictures at Yuill/Crowley gallery the year before, in a show he called *The Australian Labour Party*. The *Sydney Morning Herald*'s art critic, Bruce James, reviewed the work and was unenthused.

The paintings, however, were some of the most electric of his career: drunken koans spray-painted onto canvas or the reverse side of photographic paper, works such as *My parents telephone number is 99821626*, and later *My dad had sex with my mum*. Both paintings were no more than their titles, spelled large across the picture plane, yet they seemed to hold in a sentence all of Adam's life: a permanent adolescence, the responsibility for which was abdicated to his mother and father in suburban Collaroy. As with his earlier sculptures, he began by rebelling against materials. These were paintings against all odds. The former won the 1996 Gold Coast City Conrad Jupiters Art Prize. His father still receives phone calls to the number. "I've had about ten since he did it," Kevin says. "The bugger."

Reviewing the work, Bruce James wrote: "I find the displayed canvases flaccid, self-conscious and ungenerous.

I don't know what they mean, either – rather worrying in my position." But he found hope in a portfolio of drawings by Adam, shown elsewhere in the gallery: "[They show] all the communicative life lacking elsewhere. Truth, wit and even artistic taste leak from them like a juice."

James became an important critic of Adam's work. A year after dismissing Adam's first paintings, he wrote about the film *Inappropriate Elation* – a home video of a playground rocking horse being jolted wildly back and forth. His preface had the nervousness critics reserved for Adam's early work. It was "an acquired taste", James warned. The work could be "offensively ham-fisted" from a man "who put the faux in faux-naivety". But he also saw for the first time Adam's "gift for clowning", and called the video "Sydney's laugh of the month".

What confounded critics about Adam's work was its simplicity. Few could accept that he painted what he meant: there was no hidden meaning, no deeper purpose. If he tried for one in his thesis, it was fitted retrospectively, tongue in cheek. These were pictures of pathetic men and smudged women, painted because that is what he saw on television and in magazines. Save for his Archibald entries and a few other exceptions, Adam almost never painted from life. His pictures were transcriptions. The text was harvested from popular culture, lifted from late-night television: phrases repeated aloud, over and over, until they had either shed or gained meaning. There was no judgement and little empathy. He disliked the term "Loserville", coined for the universe in which his subjects existed: the name was often attributed to him, but it had in fact originated in an essay on his work by Ingrid Periz. "I don't think of them as losers," he said. "I don't think of them at all."

By the time James reviewed Adam's 1998 show, *World Fantasy*, he saw "an artist of real merit". James was among the first to recognise that the meaning of Adam's work sat on its surface, that he had no opinion of his subjects, good or bad: "Cullen's abjectness is not luxury at ease; his emptiness is not profundity; when he scribbles, his poor syntax is not a form of epigram. His crudeness is what it is – unabashed ... He's a bottom-feeder, none too pernickety about taste. Every pond needs one, especially the cesspools of popular culture."

A year later, James paid Adam the substantial compliment of a catalogue essay for his show at the Institute of Modern Art in Brisbane and Adelaide's Experimental Art Foundation. He was, like a number after him, convinced.

*

Adam resented other artists. He lived outside their world and often thought them weak. Occasionally, he would make a brief but intense friendship, as with the painter Ben Quilty. But his phone calls would quickly become too much and his demands too taxing – the overtures to come immediately on unplanned hunting trips, to pick up grenades for him from a store on George Street or heroin from a man in Darlinghurst. Other times, Adam would watch a career from afar, envying its achievements. He was never ashamed to express this, raging that he should have been selected for the Venice Biennale in place of Shaun Gladwell. "They should be approaching me," he said. "I was making that work ten years ago, carrying around roadkill. He lives in fucking Potts Point. I am Mad Max."

Despite his accolades, Adam always felt an outcast. He could never stand another person's success. "Artists are fucking wankers and it's almost embarrassing to be one," he said one night after a burst of painting in his studio. "I suppose I'm just very disappointed with other artists. They are all wankers – male and female. They just don't get that they will hit this wall and will be fucked. They haven't hit their head against the wall of existence like I have. They just don't understand what life is about. With art, when you're making something completely fucking useless, you can lose your sense of play. But for me everything is fun. If I lose that sense of play, I would just die or fade away. I love it because it's so useless. It's the most indulgent thing you can do, to make art. It's so fucking selfish and I love it. I reckon I'm worth eight thousand dollars an hour, and the rest."

*

Adam did not talk much about influences. The art books he bought were tattoo magazines. He made a mischief from agreement: whatever meaning a critic proposed for a work, he would concur with it. Questions about art had to be open-ended or else the answers would be useless. "In my twenties it was Kippenberger and Goya and performance art – Joseph Beuys," he said of the artists who shaped his early work. "Not necessarily the intent, but the work itself was so new and aesthetic and human and dead. It was all about death, a 'good death.'"

Among Australian artists, Nolan and Mike Parr were the only figures he consistently respected. "I'm just really interested in how he looks at colour. It's very helpful," he said of Nolan. "I don't think he was ever a very good drawer, whereas I really, really enjoy it and get a lot out of it. I really do think an artist hits his prime in his older years. Nolan has come to me late in life, or as late as my life has allowed."

*

A few weeks after Adam died, the Art Gallery of New South Wales hung his painting *Comedic relief* in its main hall. It is not a great Cullen, but nor is it a bad one. A craggy male head looms forward beside a bound figure. Everything is set in hastily mixed Dulux. The picture entered the collection via the proceeds of a dinner to mark Adam's 2008 retrospective – bought not with one generous sum but with the dribs and drabs of thirty donations; two of them from his art dealers, another from Lucy Turnbull. It seemed telling: this was a man no longer capable of mustering singular enthusiasm.

The gallery owns better examples of his work – his morally ambiguous *Portrait of John Travers*, named as the ringleader in the rape and murder of Anita Cobby; the calamitous epic *Lets get lost* – but *Comedic relief* was a fitting tribute. It was a capable depiction of Australian impotence, unsentimental in its outlook, laced with what would become Adam's plainest mannerisms: brisk drawing; spray-painted antennae, so his subject might better interpret the world; drip marks cultivated by rotating the picture while it was still wet.

This would be the first time a wall plaque for Adam had an end point: "Adam Cullen, Australia, 1965–2012." It gave the work a greater power than it might otherwise have had. Already, the explanatory text was making excuses – trying to defend through euphemism a legacy tarnished by ten years of uneven painting, by the fact that the indifference which had been the strength of Adam's work also meant he struggled to pick a good picture from a bad one. "Adam Cullen was a unique and larger-than-life figure in contemporary Australian art," it began. "His public persona obscured to a certain extent his significant contribution to art practice ... The pathos of his subject matter also has a form of abject beauty, the beauty of the decayed and coming apart, of a humanity that is to be found in failed endeavours, misunderstandings and missed connections."

*

Adam's final artistic controversy was a painting of Christ, made for the Blake Prize in 2008. The picture's inclusion among the finalists forced the resignation of one of the judges, Christopher Allen, who accused the picture of an aesthetic bluff. To be sure, it was shoddily painted and offered no reason for its garishness. "I've never even met him – I just don't like his work," Allen said. "It has a kind of deliberate ugliness which has been exploited as a gimmick. This isn't a personal preference, it's a judgement."

The resignation made the cover of the *Sydney Morning Herald* and was reported by the BBC. The work was later defended as a feminist reading of the Bible, on the basis of an inscription in the lower left-hand corner: "Only woman bleed." This was not its intention; nor had been controversy.

The picture was painted the evening before it was due in Sydney, without time for the background to dry ahead of work commencing on the foreground. Adam's paints were rotten in their cans, as they often were. They had separated and congealed. As he fixed Jesus to the cross, copying the figure from a Velázquez poster, he could not get his red acrylic to adhere. “More blood,” he repeated over and over. “More blood.” Standing in the studio, I joked that the problem was addressed in a song by Alice Cooper, “Only Women Bleed”. By this stage a bottle of vodka had been drunk and the phrase was misspelt onto the canvas. Adam had a gift for success through accident. “Sometimes I think all I have to do is wake up in the morning,” he told the *Sydney Morning Herald* at the time. “I just have to fart and there’s flames.”

A sub-editor later called to be reassured that the quote was genuine.

MOTHER

"I was fourteen when I stopped loving my mother."

The eulogy with which Adam buries his mother is written the morning of her funeral, on the back of his father's old Spanish homework. On the reverse, a series of exercises had asked Kevin to describe his family. "Carmel is the boss of the home," he wrote in gently corrected Spanish. "My eldest son, Mark, is short and fat with no hair. He lives alone in Lithgow. My youngest son, Adam, is bald, slim, very intelligent and lives in the mountains."

The worksheet also asked Kevin to describe himself, using as many adjectives as possible. He wrote: "I am seventy-two years. I have grey hair and blue eyes. The teeth are mine." Further on, he is asked to describe someone in the third person. Kevin wrote: "My friend Chopper Read is tall, big, ugly and dangerous. His body is tattooed completely. He has no ears and teeth of steel."

Adam's eulogy starts with a single word, given a line of its own, a sense of beginning with the end: "Death." In the church he lets it hang in the air, pleased with his baritone and its resonance. He liked the sound his boot heels made on the timber rise as he walked up to the pulpit. You could hear this in his deliberate footsteps. There is a pause before he continues. "Death," he says, "makes angels of us all." In angered biro he had scratched out the next line: "Mum didn't have to die." Each word is scribbled over, then long arcs slice through the whole sentence.

He continues: "Mum always was an angel. She was a great mother to my brother and I and a fine wife to my father. My memories of Mum now are from childhood. Now that she's passed on I feel as if I've been reduced to a child again. Infancy and the love of a mother. My mum was a very talented potter and actress – at times she sacrificed both to be with us – she always put family first. So this is how I see today: a celebration, a celebration of an amazing life. I love you, Mum. Forever."

*

Adam looked mostly like his mother and inherited from her his pattern baldness and his weight. Carmel had a comfortable Black Irish face. Her hairline ran high on her forehead in a perfect half-moon that was mirrored by the arc of her jaw. It was a large face, made for smiling. Adam's was as well, although he took more pleasure in holding off a grin – waiting for the person with whom he was talking to become nervous before allowing the joke to arrive on his face, bringing to the conversation a sense of relief.

Carmel's forehead was frequently shortened by the eyebrows she raised in mock surprise. She underlined points by opening her eyes very wide and had the strong presence of a matriarch used to being heard. Although she played blousy maternal figures in a handful of soap operas, she was cast mostly in comic roles. She would be a Greek on SBS – indeed, she was cast a Greek in the television series *The Girl from Steel City* and the 1975 film *Promised Woman* – and then the shoe-dwelling old woman of an Arnott's biscuit commercial.

At school, Adam was proud of this: "It was good having a mum on TV because kids thought you were cool." He would boast to other boys of her fame, and insinuate that he had relationships with actresses. But he was always uneasy with his pride. "She was in *The Benny Hill Show* when they made an Australian special," he said. "In the credits she was listed as the 'Embarrassingly Fat Woman'."

It was not until she died that Adam admitted he actually loved his mother. Certainly, his love was never unconditional. At her wake a cousin confided to me that the family had worried over what he might say at the funeral. When she had become sick with leukemia, her deterioration had only heightened what he detested in her.

She was, among other things, never pretty enough for Adam. "She's just this strange, pale, skeletal, sagging head with wispy, white hair combed back and plopped on top of a tent dress,' he said once. 'The O'Loughlan clan: they're all such fucking weirdoes."

*

The first time Adam mentions his mother to me, he says she didn't breastfeed him. This seems important to him, a kind of glib epigraph for the relationship that followed. The milk was too rich, so the child was put on formula. "I just never took to the love of a mother. I couldn't stomach it," Adam says. "I never have, really – I've never had that connection."

Nursing became a semi-regular theme in Adam's work. He liked to talk about what he called "monetary/mammary" transactions. In *Human Milk*, a monkey-headed woman stands naked beside the sign that gives the painting its title. She has cherry-red nipples and childless hips. A string of sausages below, cut in several places and labelled with the words "gene splicing", hints at Adam's increasing sense of disconnection from the world. In *Actual re-enactment*, scraps from Adam's notebooks are writ large across three panels: a fax number, the track list from an album of golfing songs, taxonomy charts. Over the final panel the words "warm mammary war" are spray-painted in thick black text.

In his mind at least, Adam's childhood rejection of breast milk cemented the myth he had built of his father as heroic provider. Adam's difficulties loving his mother were always an excuse to love his father more: "Dad made eight pounds a week and spent three pounds on my formula." It also fed his belief that some intractable feud existed between Carmel and him. "I don't know why she hates me so much," he said. "She didn't even have to breastfeed me."

*

When Carmel met Kevin, she was the single mother of a seven-year-old son. He was a recent widower, she was abandoned. "When Dad's first wife died, there was a lot of shame in that because they had been married for eighteen months," Adam said, shortening the marriage by two and a half years. "Then he married a Catholic who drank and had a son, and that's just not done if you're a Proddy. It just ostracised our family. They leave the bush, go and live in the city: who the fuck do they think they are?"

Carmel O'Loughlan was born 350 kilometres south of Kevin, in a tent outside Gundagai. From Wagga Wagga she studied by correspondence with an outfit called the London College of Drama, and as a teenager convinced her truck-driver father to move to Sydney so she could pursue a career in acting. She took singing lessons and got work at the Independent Theatre in North Sydney. But it was the tent in which she was born that made Adam proudest of his mother, and he frequently showed a black and white photograph of it. "My mother was born in a fucking tent," he said, "and now she's on TV."

Carmel met Kevin in 1962, the year his first wife died. A year later they were married. "My first wife died and I didn't care about anything much. Didn't care about anything," Kevin said. "Then I met Carm and it was good again. Carm was a bad woman. She had a seven-year-old son and she was an actress and she drank red wine and she was a Catholic. But I didn't care. You can get a good woman anytime; I wanted a bad one."

*

Adam's feud with his mother intensified in 2007, when he was hospitalised with pancreatitis. The inflammation of the pancreas, which went on to affect most of Adam's internal organs, is usually caused by alcohol abuse or gallstones. Adam didn't have gallstones. Life had caught up with him, and he was wounded by the lack of sympathy it brought when it arrived.

"She wasn't much help at all," he said of his mother. "She was a pain in the arse. She was hardly a tower of strength. She was actually whingeing at my bedside. She couldn't do anything, and Mum is someone who has got to be needed. She has got to be needed. She's great; she's a really loving mum if she's needed. Otherwise, she's a whingeing, close-minded piece of shit."

There were two predictable themes when Adam talked about his mother. Her intelligence was the first: "She was too stupid, too narrow-fucking-minded." The second was his sense of the competition between them as artists. He felt a curious guilt that she had sacrificed her career to be a mother, yet he was vicious with his own success: "She was a bitch. 'Why has Adam done this? Why is Adam doing this?

Why did Adam let this happen?' It's all about her. Sorry, Mum: it's me on the fucking flyer. Mum has no sense of putting her feelings aside. She's been wrongly done by because I'm successful. That's fucking success."

It was only after Carmel died that he confessed what he had craved: a love more unconditional, more praise for his career. "Now that she's gone, it hurts more," Adam said a month after her funeral. "There's certain things she never said that I just wanted her to say. It was like Dad had to say it for her. Things like 'I respect you for how you think and what you do'. She never, ever said that. I know she was always there for me, but she just wouldn't say it. She just wouldn't fucking take that next step."

*

Puberty did it, and Adam never recovered. "I was fourteen when I stopped loving my mother," he said late one night. "As a teenager she didn't progress, and I did. Everything I pushed, she pushed back. She always had to side with my brother, who's always been very conservative and stupid. We were very close at one time, but she just has a martyr complex. She just complains all the time. She's been very, very critical of me. She's been supportive, but very critical at the same time. It's so difficult."

Adam's trouble with his mother was inextricably tied to the hatred he felt for his half-brother, Mark. For a time he worried he was adopted, until he realised it was Mark whom Kevin had taken in. "I had a fair idea but I never asked. I was actually afraid to. I didn't want to be rejected for knowing too much. When I was eight or nine, it clicked."

In Adam's telling, his mother was eighteen when she met a soldier in his early thirties and fell pregnant with Mark. At times Adam would claim the man was a Nazi. He said his brother had no interest in the identity of his father and that the soldier knew nothing of the child.

The truth is the man was a German ship jumper – a dark-haired steward named Werner – who made Carmel pregnant while she was working at the Independent Theatre. The couple married, in line with her family's wishes, and moved to Melbourne looking for work with the 1956 Olympics. Sick from pregnancy, Carmel returned to Sydney. In Melbourne, Werner sold the young family's possessions and disappeared. "Eventually the police grabbed him because he was an illegal and he was a wife starver, which was a criminal offence," Kevin said. "The police asked Carmel, 'What do you want to do with him?' And she whispered in response, 'Put him in jail.'"

*

Adam's resentment of his brother manifested in fantastical stories, bitter and mostly fabricated. He said Mark bored people at parties; that he was a bisexual, "the most evil thing there is". He said Mark married a stripper in Potts Point, but she left him because he was too boring. He said Mark couldn't ride a bicycle.

"He and Mum gang up on me," Adam said. "That's why I left home. I have no love for him at all. He's a complete spastic. I think I just completely frustrate him because he can't understand me. I mean, how could he? He just has no critical hardware.

"Once I hit puberty, the war began because I wasn't his little brother anymore. He was a cunt. He was a very conservative prick. Just a square. Every time I'd get my hair cut, he'd say, 'You look like one of those dumb pricks me and my mates beat up.' Then the shit hit the fan when I got my nose pierced in high school. He's really old-fashioned in all of the bad ways. And he's very aggressive and fucking scared."

Hating his brother was important to Adam in the same way that rejecting Carmel's nursing had been: it allowed him to be closer to Kevin. The two boys did not speak to each other at their mother's funeral. "It was a horror story," Adam said. "I was with Dad; Mark was with Mum."

*

Women fare worse than men in Adam's paintings. They are the victims of greater violence. If his men are impotent, his women are visions of cartoon sex – gin club floozies or wild squalls of genitalia. Their faces are watery, their features barely held together with make-up.

The recurrent woman is a headless figure with smallish feet and mothering breasts. She is a silvery presence in the painting *Shut up, nobody wants to hear your stories*, all stomach and meaty arms. Her nipples have been spray-painted an angry bitten red, and some enamel has dripped where her head was severed. The patrician face beside her has been painted with greater haste, but the care with which she has been described is more mocking. Each fold of flesh is cruelly drawn, her pubic hair a comic thatch. "I've never painted any woman but my mother," Adam says. "That's her."

Carmel kept two paintings of Adam's in the front room of the house where he grew up. There was a dining table under a lacework tablecloth, and a buffet along one wall in which she stored clippings of Adam's press in ring-binder folders. Windows opened out onto a tree tied with white netting to protect it from the birds.

The pictures – a competent still life on board and a muddy homage to the Heidelberg School – were done while Adam was still at high school. Both seemed promising but unexceptional, stilted by their earnestness. Carmel pointed to the paintings with a mixture of pride and affection. She had a stoic acceptance of the man Adam became, but she was obviously still in love with the boy he had once been. When Adam arrived, he was furious to find us looking at these pictures.

"I love her, but you just have to keep things nice and simple," he said later. "She can be embarrassing at art openings. She can really embarrass herself, and me: 'Adam used to paint really well. I don't know why he paints this.' She's so jealous because I have the career she fucked up in."

Carmel turned up at a talk Adam was giving at the Hazelhurst Regional Gallery soon after we met. From the audience she asked if he ever made more realistic work. "I cut her off like she was someone who wasn't related, but she pushed the point. That fucked me off," he told me. "She wanted recognition. She wanted recognition for inspiring me to be a realistic drawer. It was absurd. She didn't understand. She felt so bad I made it because I wasn't like her. But she took credit for who I was, she just could never admit it. She was such a sensitive cow. She just wouldn't understand, she couldn't fucking do it ... She never told me how good I'd done. She never just said, 'That's so great.' Not once. Not fucking once. I only heard that I was the bad guy."

*

Adam was ten when the pictures he was drawing at school saw him referred to a psychiatrist. They were slapstick jokes mainly, but teachers worried at them. "I was taken to a shrink, and they took along all of my drawings – all these violent cartoons – then they accused my parents of hitting me. This shrink just didn't know talent when she saw it."

About the same time, Adam began to believe his father was having affairs, although this never happened. Adam imagined some sort of contract existed between his parents, sealed by his birth: his father would marry his mother and take in Mark, but only on the proviso he could continue seeing other women. Adam never confronted his father about this – perhaps because he knew it was a story of his invention, a fantasy he had built to distance himself from his mother. Still, he maintained until his death that it was true.

"He bought the deal," Adam said. "I can never understand that, but he bought the deal. He does what he wants. That is the deal. I think that's why Mum resents me so much."

*

Carmel had made a frittata with chorizo and sweet chilli sauce. Adam was not answering his phone and we started lunch without him. "He was very lucky to be able to do what he did. I found it very frustrating at times," Carmel said of his career. "We didn't say, 'You've got to get a job.' We did that with Mark. He had to get a job. He wanted to go on the music trail, but we were old-fashioned. By the time Adam was at that age, we realised the art was it. By the time he was in his teens, we knew it was best to let him do what he wanted."

Kevin interrupted: "Adam moved along in his life with a very quick development. He was unrestricted; I wouldn't say controlled. Let me tell you about Carmel. Adam wanted a motorbike. I was dead against it. Carmel is wiser than I. She said, 'Let him get a motorbike, but make sure he gets a safe one.' We didn't restrict him, but we guarded him."

Carmel eased the conversation towards her career. It was the great source of strife between her and her son, and in her gentle way she made clear that some of the resentment Adam complained of was real – amplified by his capacity for myth, but still there. "I only did work that wouldn't interfere with our home life. If I had a job, I couldn't put any make-up on because Adam would muck up all day trying to get me to take it off. I did restrict what I did. I never did theatre work, because I had to be here. I did restrict myself quite a bit. Adam didn't like me being anywhere but here. I hid what I was doing and only did jobs in school hours. He started pre-school, but he only lasted a day."

Carmel poured herself a drink. By now Adam had missed lunch. "It was incredible how fast Adam did these things," Carmel continued. "We just got a phone call and he would be back here. But he ended up at this psychiatrist who said we were hitting him: that I must be an actress and be away all the time. He didn't draw for six months after that, but he said he wouldn't go back."

Adam arrived and Kevin got up to greet him in the kitchen. Carmel pushed on, anxious to finish the conversation before he reached the table. “I didn’t want to mix with the acting fraternity because I didn’t get any satisfaction out of that,” she said, tempering her previous statements, keen to show how she had nurtured his creativity. “All I know about Adam is that he always had a pen or a brush or pencil in his hand. I’d sort of paint, but I would never tell him not to join in. He was very happy doing that sort of thing.”

*

“Excuse my call of urgency,” Adam begins our first conversation of 2010. “My parents are sort of ageing and stuff. Mum’s dying and Mark is just the biggest cunt. He won’t even call Mum. She’s dying and he won’t even fucking call her.”

Chemotherapy had made Carmel too sick for Christmas. A stroke had taken the sight in one of Kevin’s eyes and left him unable to drive for a time. For Adam, Carmel’s sickness was about Kevin. He said his father now did all the cleaning at home, that when his mother tried to cook, it took her an hour to peel a potato. But there was sudden concern in his voice at losing the woman he claimed not to have loved for thirty years. “It’s all happened so fast. I don’t think they’re handling the change so well. I suppose they’re apprehensive about all these changes all of a sudden. Their whole life is based around appointments and seeing people and being healthy. I hope they can just hop over this first hurdle and settle into some sort of routine where it’s not so demanding the whole time. Carm's always been so needy, but Kevin's suddenly lost his independence. In short, they're fine: they're enduringly indestructible."

He worried about their ability to keep his childhood home. He often said he would go back to live there, and ranted about his brother's imagined intention to sell the house Kevin had built. "They've had a few fights because Dad changed the will. I don't know the contents, but I think it's to do with what happens with Mark and the house. Dad built every structure in that house. It should be a mausoleum: his castle. I told Dad it should stay with me and not be sold. The only time they fight is over Mark."

*

The last time I saw Carmel, she was bald. I mentioned what Adam had told me about his own baldness, acquired during a teenage dalliance with skinhead culture and worn through adulthood. "I started shaving my head when I was seventeen," he had said. "And then, when I stopped, I was bald."

By the time Adam left home, he was frequenting the Harold Park Hotel in Glebe. His bald head and cherubic face made him stand out among the elderly drinkers. He was an oddity, and he enjoyed it. "Adam used to tell them he had leukemia and they gave him free beer," Carmel said. "Now I've bloody got it. He gave it to me."

*

Adam cried a lot when his mother finally died. He was in Karratha painting for a show when he heard the news. "I'm not really all that well," he said when he called to tell me. "Mum's dead. I'm not that concerned about her. I'm just concerned about my old man. He was in tears when he told me. He just said, 'She's gone.' I was in fucking tears. All I said was, 'Oh shit. Oh shit.' What else do you say? I was in this lonely hotel room in the desert and I get a call from a grieving man telling me my fucking mum's dead? Her corpse had the strangest smile on its face. It looked like she was taking the piss."

The diary he kept at the time was a stubby Moleskine that smelt faintly of sour cranberry juice, as did everything in his house. He often kept more than one diary a year because he filled them faster than was allowed for by the ordinary passing of time. Appointments would tumble forward through weeks. Lists would re-emerge each month, reordered but still uncompleted.

The diary announces itself with a sad-eyed sketch of a clown, above which Adam has written the words "Beelze Bobo" – a childish bastardisation of the devil Beelzebub. Ten pages later, he writes in bold capitals, "The planet will fuck itself in … 2016." All of Adam's diaries are full of such predictions – "Adam Cullen will die in 2018" – and they almost always appear in the first few pages, as if to curse the rest of the book.

The remainder of the diary progresses as they mostly do, with a series of schoolboy cartoons and fanciful inventions: a fatted portrait of Mary MacKillop; a design for an electric helmet; various naked men; the snuffling trunked heads of imagined megafauna. The words to 'Come On Eileen' by Dexys Midnight Runners are written across the entries for 23 and 25 June.

On 14 July 2010 he draws no pictures. In uncharacteristically loose lettering he writes a single sentence: "Mum died today." The word "died" is underscored by a slow, deep line that cuts into the paper. The following day, in capitals, his entry reads: "My mother died yesterday." The page is marked with a red stamp that spells "Fuck Off" in block letters. The same stamp has been applied to the previous six days, although not to the day Carmel died. It is stamped forward in the diary for another seventeen pages.

There is mournful repetition to the next month. He writes "Mum's dead" on 17 July. "Dead and gone" on 19 July. On 21 July, simply "Dead". A coffin appears on 23 July. A Petrine cross begins entering the diary on 25 July: the inverted symbol of Christ, used by Catholics as a sign of unworthiness and later co-opted into Satanism and the predictable iconography of heavy metal.

On 31 July the cross is replaced by a single word, almost illegible, rendered in a hand that is unmistakably drunk: "Mummy."

DRUGS

"If I wasn't sick, this would be a great holiday."

Adam was always dying. He called once to say he had pancreatic cancer, although it turned out to be a scare. His prognosis improved little either way. In the last years of his life he was in hospital every other month. Drugs wore away at each part of him. The stents in his ducts failed frequently, flooding his body with bile, washing him an awful yellow. "I look like an A-rab," he would say, coming down hard on the first syllable. "A fucking A-rab."

But Adam enjoyed hospitals. He was healthiest when he was sick. A call would come from the ward at the Nepean, praising the food and asking for cigarettes. Stuyvesant Red, soft pack. Other friends would courier in heroin for him. "I'm in hospital," he would joke, "and I still have to look after my own fucking pain relief."

In reality, hospitals gave Adam what he craved most: the sense somebody cared. "I actually really enjoy hospital. They actually care for you, and it's really rather nice. It's great, actually. I draw and I think about my own mortality. I'm not here for long, but I'm certainly going to get my kicks until the whole fucking treehouse burns up in flames."

*

David Attenborough's *The Life of Mammals* is playing on a television. It is the monkey episode, about forming social groups. A baby in a highchair sits in front of the screen. From the toys on the floor it is clear there is a toddler somewhere too. Adam is expecting his dealer to open the door, but it is his dealer's wife who answers. He kisses her on the cheek and walks into the kitchen. Torn books and tied bags of garbage are piled up in the corners of the house. The couch is lost beneath unfolded laundry.

Adam's dealer takes him upstairs. The heroin he is here for is stuffed into the cut-off corners of shopping bags, twisted at the top to make little pouches. Adam undoes one and with a shaking hand coaxes the yellowish rocks into a spoon. He carries his syringes and cotton buds and saline capsules and teaspoon in an old wooden box that once held Winsor & Newton watercolours. A tourniquet he stole from his last hospital stay is fetched from his jacket pocket.

The dealer fixes himself a taste as Adam dissolves the smack over the heat of his lighter. Downstairs, the baby is crying. Oil floats to the top of the heroin. "Sorry about that," the dealer says. "It's from Guam."

Adam rolls up his sleeve and ties off. His jacket arms are never buttoned. He draws up the hit through an ear of cotton wool and hunts his forearm for a vein. "I always liked a challenge," he says. The truth is his major veins are useless – collapsed after years of injecting. Adam misses twice, but on the third attempt he hits something and watches as a whisper of blood enters the syringe's chamber and mingles with the yellow junk. "I never did anything the easy way."

A taxi is waiting outside, having driven Adam from Wentworth Falls to the housing estate on Sydney's western fringe. As soon as he is inside the car, he lights a cigarette. Adam only travels with drivers who will let him smoke. "It's about getting lost," he is saying as the smack kicks in. "Lost in jazz, lost in heroin, just being free ..."

By the time the taxi finds the freeway, Adam is on the nod. His cigarette falls from his fingers and burns a small hole in the denim jacket he is wearing. The driver waits until the McDonald's at Blaxland to prod him awake. Adam orders a coffee: white with three sugars. This is a familiar trip and the driver follows it to order. All up, it takes about three hours. Adam picks up the conversation as if he had never been asleep: "I own a gun, I take drugs, I'm fucking free – just free, free, free."

Taxi drivers fight for Adam's fare. It is a $300 wait-and-return, and he takes the ride three times a week.

*

Adam started smoking marijuana when he was fourteen but graduated to speed as soon as he made it off the Northern Beaches. That was six months into art school. "I used to shoot the fucking speed and it was awful," he said. "That shit was toxic, it was really fucking toxic." Not that the marijuana stopped. He was living in Annandale with a man whose parents had a farm outside Lismore: the supply was too attractive. "He'd bring down a garbage bag of dope he called Water Hen. It grew on the edge of a swamp. One toke and you'd be fucked. It made him very popular with me for about two years."

Adam used heroin for the first time at twenty-one, in the toilets of the Marlborough Hotel in Newtown. It was a defining evening – a "little taste from a little Mick". He never really stopped. "I started taking heroin when I was trying to get off speed. I was into uppers and I could handle the uppers, but I had to go down somehow. Go down, just go down."

*

In June 2008 Adam announces he is quitting. This happens periodically. He has watched Andrew Denton interviewing Dame Elisabeth Murdoch, the 99-year-old matriarch of the News Corp media dynasty, and decided he wants to live as long as she did. "She is the most beautiful old girl I've seen. It gave me an epiphany," he says in a car outside the Art Gallery of New South Wales, where he has been signing books. "I've been to rehab about four times, but it never really works. I just don't want to end up in some fucking old man's home like Max did."

Adam's second cousin, the actor Max Cullen, had been in Ireland when he found himself in a doss house, wet with drink, fleeing a broken marriage and a long affair and another short one. Adam had met Max for the first time the day before he left, during a family reunion at the Carrington Hotel in Katoomba. He was fourteen. The episode that followed for Max had always troubled him. "I guess I just think everything's a party, and it's not," Adam says. "I am an old man and I've just got to stop the booze."

The story only begins to make sense when Adam stops the car at a teller machine on Oxford Street. He needs to borrow $600 from me, and he doesn't want me to know he is using it to score.

*

"Extreme intoxication, I suppose, was a method of coping," Adam said. "I was self-medicating at a very early age. I loved being with my dad, but I was into things that people don't really approve of. It was a way of hiding from people. I used to hide a lot – a hell of a lot."

Adam could not explain addiction without mentioning dislocation, then pain relief. Drugs began as a rebellion but soon became a salve for his loneliness. Adam worked hard to isolate himself, then struggled to fill the void left by the absence of other people. "There was a band called the

Anti-Nowhere League," he said, trying to explain an adolescence he never properly outgrew. "They had a song called 'I Hate People', and I had a T-shirt with 'I Hate People' written on it. I was seventeen – just a fucking boy – and my mother fucking hated it."

Adam rarely painted without first finishing a bottle of vodka. He would often shoot up on the couch before heading to the studio. When Adam said he was hiding, it was not from life but from his talent. He was terrified by the prospect of being judged sober. Drugs were a crutch he finally couldn't work without. "I suppose it puts some protection there," he confessed one night. "It puts some space between me and the work, and I think I need that."

He also liked the myth – the cadre of artists into which heroin put him. Some nights he would call himself the next Brett Whiteley; other times it would be Hunter S. Thompson or William S. Burroughs, whom he called Bill. He felt drugs put him in contact with a reality hidden from other people, that they made his story interesting, that they added complexity to an uncomplicated childhood. Drugs were a paradox for Adam: a way of staying in touch with the reality of the street while he put himself out of touch with the realities of life.

"A person has to go to the street – the street to find things, the street to talk, the street for relief. We all have to go," he said. "I'm not a junkie. I don't look like a junkie. I don't talk like a junkie. I'm not a junkie, but if you want help you have to go get it. It's not something I think about, but if I can get it I will. It's the best pain relief ever."

*

It was in Hill End, outside Bathurst, that Adam identified the first signs of the pancreatitis that eventually filleted him, taking his gallbladder and cutting significant portions from several other organs. The year was 2007. "I was drinking and confused and really bitter," he said. "It was something I didn't think of as my fault. I thought, 'Why me?' I was absolutely indestructible."

The location said a lot about Adam's myth: he wanted to think of himself as the last of the wild colonials, but an artist residency in the gold town had shown him he did not belong. He was not made for the bush, and nor was the bush what he thought it would be. "I was going up there for R&R, and all I did was shoot and ride and drink and ride horses around like a drunk bushranger riding around with a fucking sidearm," he said. "I got back and I woke up one morning feeling like I'd been shot in the chest. No, in the guts. Basically, I wasn't around people who really liked me very much. They were basically very scared of me. I'm not pissing in my own pocket, but I was an intellectual. I didn't befriend anyone up there. I certainly didn't make friends with the publican. The head barman was a prick. He'd cut you, but it wasn't any of his own business. I spent a lot of time drinking alone. That was my choice. I was out all day and up all night."

Even as he told the story – and he told it always with bitterness – he was warming to the circumstances. Foremost in Adam's mind was his conviction in the power of experience. "I think you understand things when you live them, otherwise it's still just an idea – just a fucking idea," he said. "People don't understand the agony I've endured through that operation. My surgeon said it would kill most people, but I'm still alive. I suppose that's why I throw myself around; I suppose I just don't care anymore. It's not immortality but mortality: I actually know how close I can get."

*

In his final years Adam uses the black-market narcotic OxyContin and keeps a prescription to the Methadone-like opioid Physeptone. He is also injecting heroin.

We drive to three different houses in Katoomba, looking to score. The taxi waits out front of each. Most of the dealers on whom Adam relies are users themselves, and the supply is unreliable. He finally gets a sheet of OxyContin. Adam is adamant he needs the drug to relieve pain in his abdomen, but he crushes the pills and injects them like smack. "I still have to get my kicks somehow," he says. "People don't want you to have fun, but I want to have fun."

The first pancreatitis operation left Adam with forty-two stitches snaking the length of his abdomen: "I could feel every one, tearing at my guts – raw flesh stitched together with these staples, just waiting to tear open."

His weight dropped to fifty-two kilograms: "All I was focused on was staying alive, which was a big thing considering I had never done that ... I went from being a guy who thought he was great to being this piece of shit. A shrink told me I have what soldiers have: PTSD."

For the first time, he started using antidepressants seriously: "I tried three courses in about eight months, then I stopped. It just makes me impotent and constipated and flat. I didn't want to have any fun. I didn't want to go out. I didn't want to go out because people are boring. Australia is so fucking boring. You can't say this, you can't do this. There's all these fucking laws. I arose from the dead but not as the same person: I'm not the same person. I'm not as accepting. I'm not as forgiving. I'm a little bit less tolerant of most things. I look after myself. I'm a little bit more self-concerned."

Survival made Adam boastful. Concern from others made him feel wanted. He likened himself to Prometheus, living recklessly for the benefit of those less brave, stealing from the gods to give mortals fire: "I sold more work in those three months in hospital than I've ever sold. I made $300,000 – $100,000 a month – because people thought I was dead. I was loaded in hospital: loaded with money and loaded with morphine. It was fucking amazing. It was such a great experience, a great Promethean experience. I felt like some dying Caesar."

Even after the operation, Adam did not stop using. If anything, the pain made him use more: "I put myself through a test. I'm still harming myself. Not as much as I used to. I was as sober as a judge and it was as boring as bat-shit. I've never been bored. I've never said, 'Mum, I'm bored.' I was never one of those kids."

*

Adam loved overstatement. He couldn't help himself. Lies are the first and most enduring symptom of addiction. He told me once that he had been the driver in the Nugan Hand Bank murder. His interest in crime always helped along his interest in drugs. He liked that both were illicit: it made him feel special. "I can't remember the exact date, but it was March 1987," he said. "He was a bald Negro in a grey suit. I picked him up at the airport and eight hours later I dropped him back there, and I can just remember how all I could smell on him was the gunpowder."

The story was a detailed one. Adam's mostly were. "I always start conversations with people in bars," he said. "That's what a bar is for." Adam said he was twenty-one when he met Bernie Houghton, a suspected CIA-connected spy and a director of the Nugan Hand Bank, a criminal front implicated in arms trading, drug trafficking, money laundering and the financing of a war in Laos. "I didn't even know who he was. He had terrible dress sense. He used to wear these pale blue or orange cardigans. And these slightly flowery gay pants with a pleat. I think his shoes even had a brogue, and a horrible green tie and that fucking cardigan. I was imagining who this guy in this horrible cardigan – this accountant – was until he opened his mouth and this broad American accent came out. Then you knew why he wore the cardigan."

Houghton owned the Bourbon and Beefsteak in Kings Cross, an R&R bar where Adam liked to eat late breakfasts. "It was great there, because they used to cook a fantastic breakfast, and I think they had these great ex-army cooks or something," he said. "They'd make a fry-up – eggs, bacon, tomato, real American hash browns – and I would have that with a few Bloody Marys and the condiments. God, I remember they had just the best condiments – whatever you wanted."

Adam said Houghton came to like him and eventually asked him to work as a driver. He started with small jobs. Houghton let him look in on his world a little, and Adam enjoyed it. When authorities started looking too closely at the Nugan Hand Bank, Houghton asked if he would drive on a bigger job. Adam did not know it at the time, but one of the bank's directors, Frank Nugan, was to be the victim of a hit.

"I didn't really tell many people, because I couldn't. I just wanted to be the suspicious young chap who hung around there sporadically," he said. "Most people thought I was just a driver. Usually it was just picking up a crate of scotch off the docks from a guy who owed him, or picking up meat from a place down in Pyrmont. They were actually criminal-class gentlemen: they kept with their own and they didn't involve people on the street. It was probably only half a year, but it just sticks in my head – what I saw but didn't see. I didn't know how bad a lot of this was, but the shit that used to go down there …"

The story is perfect Adam. He has a gift for association, for the occasional glamour that hangs around criminals. After two royal commissions, the responsibility for Nugan's death is still uncertain. Initial investigations called it a suicide. No one has been convicted for the crime. "I always sort of tried to maintain some sort of double existence, in a way," Adam said. "But I suppose I'm not very good at it. This whole outsider thing – being outside the law but being respectable – I just think it's a very human thing to be interested in a more sort of dark side. Also, it's a fucking lot of fun. It's nice to be able to hand a copper a crate of whisky and tell him to get out of here. That's power. It's a cheap version of power, but when you're a young kid it's great."

He starts on the condiments again. "I just loved all the condiments: relishes, Worcestershire sauce, Dijon mustard, English mustard, American mustard, catsup, cranberry. They had everything."

Adam was fourteen years old in 1980 when Frank Nugan was found dead in his Mercedes outside Lithgow. "Oh," he says when I confront him with this. "Maybe it was something else."

*

Adam arrives at my twenty-first birthday party by taxi. He is skeletal, his legs like bones in empty jeans, his stomach bloated with disease.

He walks up to the painter McLean Edwards, an old friend. "Hey, dig," he says. "Looks like it's going to rain." Edwards looks at Adam. The two men have not spoken in several years. "It just did."

The meter running outside, Adam goes into the bathroom and shoots up. I am living at the time in a little house on a big block near the train line in Marrickville. For the next two hours he stands in the garden and tells my grandmother what it is like to be an artist. He calls me the next morning to rhapsodise on the importance of family. We rarely have another conversation in which he does not ask after my nan's health.

*

When Adam was first diagnosed with pancreatitis – "my pancreas was eating itself and eating my body" – he became convinced he would die. He was in bed for three months, being fed through his nose. Tubes ran out of him, draining pus and urine into bags strung around his bed. He refused to accept what was happening, that drugs and drink had caused this. And yet the dependency he felt on other people – on medicine – bruised him. He never properly regained his reckless confidence.

"It was so weird. I was incredibly dependent. I couldn't talk because my tongue was stuck to the top of my mouth, talking like a fucking retard," he said. "My arm, the side of my body – everything was so strange. I was like a puppet. I could feel my body kicking into action, trying to stay alive. I just had to touch my gown to feel pain. I craved cocktails – little green drinks with umbrellas on top. And I wanted cocktail frankfurts in a bun with sauerkraut and lots of mustard. I was just a big baby. I looked like a feeble little girl. I was so sickly, with a big head and big jaw, sickly arms and sickly little legs."

If Adam's life ended in two great indignities, this was the first. The second was his weapons case. In sketchbooks Adam started drawing himself as an anonymous figure with a leaking penis. The only distinguishing marks were the scarred drainage holes puncturing his abdomen, each drawn as a heavy X, and a line of stitches buckling the length of his stomach. "It's a pretty life-changing thing," he said of the pancreatitis. "It's affected my relationships. My body image isn't that good, my sense of self. But everyone has their own issues with self."

*

Adam is high when he calls Chopper Read. He has been watching a late session of parliament and aping the Speaker's call: "The Member for Blah Blah. The Member for Blah Blah will resume his seat."

He has decided he needs another gun and that he should call Read to get it. The two keep in steady contact after Read slipped a trip into Adam's drink while he was being painted for the Archibald Prize. They published a children's book together. Adam was the best man at Read's wedding, and is a godparent to his son. Occasionally a truck will pull up outside Adam's house with a present from Read: a gun, or a taser, or a packet of photographs.

The voice at the other end of the phone is also high. "Yes, it's Uncle Chop Chop," he says. "Been on the old Harry, have we? The Harry Houdini."

The call drops out and Adam is unable to reconnect the line. We start to talk again about drugs. I mention the home enema kit that sits on top of his toilet cistern, the constipation of opiates. Adam confesses it has been two years since he ate solids without vomiting. He can no longer digest meat. His diet is reduced mostly to milk and fruit juice. Not infrequently, he seems pathetic.

We sit for a time, him in racing stillness, in heroin's numb facsimile of death. "I need drugs," he says finally. "I don't know what it's like without them anymore."

*

The growth doctors thought was pancreatic cancer, two years after Adam's first operation, turned out to be a benign tumour on his spleen the size of a fist. While his second Melbourne show was opening at Tolarno Galleries, he was having exploratory surgery at Nepean Hospital. A stent was inserted to connect a bile duct to his spleen.

"If I wasn't sick, this would be a great holiday," Adam says. "Bed, TV, heaps of food. And excellent pain relief. I've even got a new pot plant. My father brought a bromeliad up."

For the first time, however, he says he is scared. "I don't mind them removing foreign bodies, but I don't want them taking any more organs out. I kind of want them for a bit longer. And I'm not the sort of guy that could do a bag. I would be putting the .347 into my mouth."

When I arrive with a pack of Peter Stuyvesants, he is reading Bill "Swampy" Marsh's *Great Australian Droving Stories*. Sickness made him long to be a child. He takes my notepad and sketches me. It is rudimentary, but the biro scratches in with great purpose. He spends most time on my sideburns and jaw.

"I try to take every day as it comes now," he says. "I'm starting to fade to grey. But I'm not going to ruin dying with something that might not happen. I'm not fucking dead yet and it will take a lot to kill me. It has so far and I'm not going without a fight. I'm not sure what Hunter S. Thompson would say about this, but involving friends in your own death wish is fun, dragging people into your own hellhole of adventure. I'm a ticking time bomb. I just like to push things. I just have to push it. If you push things, you know where things are: you know where you can go."

I wait outside the bathroom cubicle while Adam shoots up, then wheel him back to bed.

ARCHIBALD

"It was the best day of my life."

The call came in the morning, telling Adam he had won. He was waiting by the phone. Driving from his house in Lilyfield to the Art Gallery of New South Wales, he repeated the same phrase over and over: "I've done it. I've finally done it."

Adam was eight months clean when he finished the picture that won him the Archibald Prize. He had seen *The Boys* at the Valhalla in Glebe, was taken by David Wenham's character, and asked to paint him. Preparatory sketches were made in bars, scarring a cigarette box with a lit smoke. He sketched with a biro into wetted beer coasters. But the final work was painted from photographs, as were most of Adam's portraits.

In Wenham's isolated villain, Adam found strange affinity. He was menacing and alone, but at the same time deeply ordinary. The film's violent suburbia matched with Adam's own interests, with his belief that evil was hidden in men and in the suburbs. He liked the astriction of the plot. A man returning home from prison, his brothers waiting for him, his mother fussing over him, his malevolence both suspenseful and a mystery, his presence at the centre of the film winding an entire house with tension. In the end, the picture succeeded because it allowed Adam to paint his favourite subject: male failure. This dead-eyed figure caught, as Adam's best pictures did, the great emptiness of Australian manhood.

"Something as cheap as winning the Archibald Prize – it was the best day of my life," he said later. "I came home to my view, to all my stuff. All my bills were paid. I was alone, but I was alive. It was a complete new start."

*

Adam had scarcely begun painting when he entered the Archibald for the first time in 1996. The portrait was of Thomas Keneally, and was not hung. "He was at the same time flippant and creative. A very good combination," Keneally recalled of the sitting. "The result reminded me a lot of Nolan's *Robert O'Hara Burke*, but with a Manly jersey thrown in for free. An amiable, mischievous soul with a deceptively simple method. But try to imitate him and you see how skilful it is."

It was at a party, less than a year after this painting was rejected, that Adam spotted Mikey Robins. The comic was doing breakfast radio at the time, with a thick Irish body and hair he wore slightly long to make the most of its colour before he greyed. He fancied it made him look like Oscar Wilde. "A little shambling bloke came up," Robins recalled, "and said he'd like to paint me for the Archibald."

Robins did not know who Adam was, but he said yes. Later, he found a picture of the dead cat Adam had showed covered in packing foam and toothpaste – *The otherness when it comes* – and deemed these credentials reassuring. Robins sat twice for the picture. In the first session Adam made a few sketches and took photographs. A few days later he called and asked Robins to sit again, this time in a suit. In all, it took about half an hour. The final painting had the broadcaster looking like a doughy wedding singer, and was hung. Robins was one of the first people Adam called when he got the news: "Mate, it's in the fucking exhibition."

From there began a roll. Adam hung again in 1998, this time with a picture of the writer Frank Moorhouse. He was highly commended the following year for a toad-headed painting of Max Cullen, which he was photographed carrying into the gallery, hidden but for his bare legs and Blundstones sticking out beneath the canvas. He claimed he had been the winner until a lone trustee, the painter Jeffrey Smart, dissented in favour of Euan MacLeod. This was not true: Jeffrey Smart had never been a trustee.

*

Adam dominated the press lead-up to the 2000 Archibald. It was only the fourth time he had been selected for the exhibition, but already he was being treated as a certainty to win. Writing in the *Sydney Morning Herald*, the critic

Sebastian Smee gave his Wenham picture 3–1 odds and named it "the one to beat".

At the winner's announcement, Adam thanked "Irish luck on St Patrick's Day". He could do with the money, he said, and got a laugh. He thanked his girlfriend, Carrie, the trustees, and his dog, Growler. It had "pissed on several paintings, but not this one", he told the assembled media, "so I suppose I'll have to buy him a carcass of something".

Adam celebrated his win at the Bayswater Brasserie in Potts Point. Mikey Robins gave him a French pocketknife and put his credit card behind the bar, "full of piss and generosity". The two men embraced. It was a night of hugs and champagne. Adam smiles out of photographs from the evening, his face childlike and brimming with mischief. A cigarette hangs from his lip and his arms are wrapped around whoever is nearest him. There was a sense in the room that a big box had been ticked. "I've fucking done it, mate," Adam told Robins when he arrived. "I've fucking done it."

*

It was reported there were "fierce behind-the-scenes arguments" about Adam's win. In announcing the prize, the president of the board of trustees, David Gonski, said there had been "a very lengthy debate" between judges. Jenny Sages and Garry Shead were reportedly in contention.

But according to the gallery's director, Edmund Capon, there was no conflict. The judging proceeded as it usually did. First, packers carried the five hundred entered portraits past the gallery trustees in quick succession. These were culled to twenty-nine, which Capon then hung. Over a few days each trustee walked through the exhibition and chose five favourites and these were culled, one by one, until a winner could be decided.

"It was a good subject that Adam picked," Capon said. "Trustees are always looking to be conservatively different – and, after all, the previous winner, Euan MacLeod, was a big, dark, sonorous picture. Here was one that was fairly different. They wanted to be radical but they can't quite be really radical. It's not in their nature."

For the director, who is not involved in the judging but has a power of veto, it was a happy decision: "I loved the picture. There was something so direct and fresh. Something, as the Chinese would say, untrammelled about it."

*

Adam loved prizes. He never stopped entering them. He was a regular in the Blake and the Moran, and in smaller suburban competitions. In 2005 he won the Mosman Art Prize for an undistinguished picture of a headless surfer. "People actually booed me in the gallery," he said. "It was so great."

Prizes were a type of validation for Adam. Like a schoolboy, he was proud of them. And yet winning them also made him more of an outsider – he felt that people mocked him for the unseriousness of what he called a "horse race".

Adam wanted desperately to win the Archibald Prize. It was the focus of his career for the handful of years before the Wenham portrait. But after he won it he was morose, sometimes belligerent. "The only thing worse than being an unsuccessful artist," he told people at the time, "is being a successful artist."

*

Up until his death, Adam maintained he received weekly hate mail for the Wenham picture. It was a lie, but it told you what Adam really thought. The hate mail confirmed his claim that the decision to be a painter was a transgression which put him at odds with the contemporary art world, that he was the first of his generation to turn away from performance and installation art and to start painting. A lot in Adam's career was accidental, but being a painter was deliberate. He would often say, by way of explanation: "No one else was doing it."

Adam had nothing for the Archibald in 2001. Then came a series of corpse paintings, his ambition now dead and his subjects looking much the same: Chopper Read in 2002, who mugged for the cameras and joked that he'd almost hung once before but that was for murder; a dead Jimmy Little in 2003, when he was still alive; a very dead Margaret Throsby in 2004; and then a hiatus until the most dead of them all, Edmund Capon, arrived in 2006.

Capon sat three times for his portrait, driving his obstinate old Jaguar up the mountains after work. At the end of the third session, when Adam announced he was finished, Capon asked if he might see the canvas Adam had been sloshing at and fussing over for the past few hours. Adam agreed, and turned it to show a shining expanse of wet blue paint without a mark on it. "I've got what I wanted," he said.

Three more pictures hung after Capon, whom Adam eventually sketched from photographs as a dripping ghoul. They were of the painter Gareth Sansom, the barrister Charles Waterstreet and the filmmaker Nelson Woss. All were pastiches. Four months after the final painting was selected, Adam was dead. His father tried to sell back a suit of Kelly armour bought from his last subject, Woss, but struggled to contact him.

*

There was nothing mysterious about the way Adam chose his subjects: he either wanted to meet them, or he thought their profile would better his chance of winning. With Wenham, it was both.

When we first talk about the Archibald, we are sitting on Adam's couch. *The Proposition* is on television. It is eight years since he won the prize and we have spent the afternoon drinking. The plot of Nick Cave's fratricidal Western is too complex to pick up this far into the film, and instead Adam hunts his coffee table for a fix of heroin. David Wenham's face fills up the screen and Adam starts to rant that he should have written the script, that he would challenge Cave to a boxing match and it would be decided who better understood Australia. He calms himself with a needle. "Weno, you cunt," he says at the television. "I mean, fucking call me. Just fucking call me."

*

His Archibald win was the defining moment of Adam's career. The Wenham picture became the image with which he was most associated. Afterwards, there was little he could paint that would not sell. His celebrity expanded hugely. A hungry press grew hungrier. "It made me a professional," he said. "Kind of mainstream."

Two days after the win, the *Sun-Herald* ran a piece headlined "Diver fans flock to Archie". Adam hated it. "By yesterday morning the crowds had gathered to view the painting and most had nothing but praise, coloured by their love of the laid-back actor," the report noted. "When asked about their impressions of the portrait, women used words like 'dreamboat' and 'dishy' ... Further pressed on the merits of the actual painting, as opposed to Mr Wenham, visitors were still generally effusive, describing it as 'lively', 'child-like' and 'expressive'."

Jann Zintgraff, of Paddington, added: "He's captured the spirit of Diver Dan. There's the freedom there of someone who hasn't necessarily studied art, but it's tremendous."

Adam had painted a monster, the violent criminal of Stephen Sewell's screenplay. He was wounded when people saw instead the heart-throb of an ABC television drama – the salt-haired male lead from *SeaChange*. This was his great peak, and yet his subject was entirely misunderstood.

On radio, Richard Glover asked if the painting's big empty eyes were a window to the soul. "No," Adam said over laughter, "because I don't actually believe in a soul."

FATHER

"Da is my hero."

Adam's father was fourteen when he lost his virginity. She was an older woman, from whom his mother had sent him to buy eggs. He was an enthusiastic teenager. These isolated facts are unremarkable. Sex is the dull backbeat to the boredom of country towns. But these isolated facts marked the beginning of a manhood Adam envied his entire life. Kevin smiles even now as he tells the story, sixty-four years later: "She started me off on the track of debauchery."

*

Adam liked to say Kevin rode into Sydney on a motorcycle, although the truth was he arrived by train. Already in Adam's telling he had the nickname Flash Mick, although it would be a decade before he met Carmel and her mother gave it to him. Kevin was a short man with big hands and bouffant hair. He had a happy tic of conversation that caused him to finish every fourth sentence with the words "And that was good". His smile was marsupial, a grin that would make his moustache wiggle back and forth before it cracked over his face.

Kevin was a surfer and a builder, a story-telling country boy. He was Adam's definition of Australian manhood. "Dad's optimistic, outgoing, adventurous, fun," Adam said before introducing us. "He tells great stories." Kevin was Adam's idol and his greatest reassurance. Adam would call him daily to be told he was okay. He couldn't work without this simple reassurance. The older he became, the more he depended on it.

"I would speak to Adam every day, two or three times a day," Kevin said a few months after Adam died. "Now if the phone rings I still think, 'God, Adam. Don't ring now.' He needed contact with me for reassurance ... In his relationship with me he needed two things. First of all he needed to be reassured that I was still here and that I loved him. Also, he needed assurance that his work was good and worthwhile. I could say that by saying, 'Adam, I'm very proud of you.' And I would quote the words of Jack Gibson, the coach of Parramatta: 'Mate, you're doing well. Play hard. Take it up them.' He needed a hand, a supportive hand."

*

The Cullen family reached Australia five generations before Kevin was born. Cornelius Cullen was a ploughman and a housebreaker when he was arrested in Killinkere, a parish of County Cavan. Records described him as a thickset man, blind in one eye and with a face scarred by smallpox, sentenced to transportation for life after a robbery in 1820. It was 1822 by the time he arrived in Sydney Cove, standing above deck on the ship *Isabella.* A few years passed before his wife and seven children were brought from Ireland to live with him. From there the family tree crawled back and forth across New South Wales for a hundred and thirty years, from Campbelltown to Narromine and back again.

The version Kevin has does not reach his own birth, so he has drawn it in with careful block letters: "Kevin J. Cullen, b. 6.8.35, m. 14.9.63 Sydney, Carmel Lois O'Loughlan, b. 20.3.34 Gundagai." He has added another branch for Adam and begun adding one for Mark, although he has not remembered his date of birth and this is left blank.

Because the tree does not reach Kevin, it does not record his illegitimate older brother, Ernie. He was raised as his grandparents' son, shunned by the family and forced to eat dinner alone in the kitchen each night. It was not until he was leaving Narromine for the war that Kevin's mother told Ernie she was his mother, too. "She waited until that day on the troop train to tell him: 'Ernie, I'm not your sister. I'm your mother.' He went to war – to New Guinea, to Malaya. He came back, but Mum didn't hear from him all that time. He couldn't bring himself to forgive her, to contact her."

The Cullen line is dotted with the hardship and intrigue that runs through country Australia. Sex and death are the unspoken constants of the bush. Kevin is the youngest of five brothers. One lost a wife to suicide; another lost his son. His father, a butcher, died when Kevin was fifteen, and he cried for a month. "I still dream of Pop," he says. "I dream of him as a boy."

*

Kevin arrived in Sydney four years into a five-year builder's apprenticeship, following the girl who would become his first wife. "I was sick of Narromine. Everything was limited."

He was nineteen years old, a young man raised by big brothers, especially Mouse, whose nickname had replaced entirely his Christian name, Ron. Mouse was a georgic rooter whom Kevin worshipped, the eldest until Ernie was revealed as their brother. In Sydney Kevin boarded with an aunt and uncle – Ada and Barney – in Bellfield. His uncle threw him out, he said, for making too much noise on the motorcycle he had bought soon after arriving. And so began his stretch in boarding houses, where he learned to drink warm beer and eat cold toast. He moved nineteen times in two years.

"At nineteen you think you know everything, but you know fuck all," Kevin said. "Ada would sit and talk to me. She was a friendly ear and had the most beautiful breasts I'd witnessed. I could just scoop them out. Bad thoughts, you see. Just like Mouse."

As he told me this, I recalled one of the last things

Carmel said to me before she died: "Mouse was an idiot, a complete bloody idiot."

*

Adam was three when he drew a jar of sweets and it became obvious he was somehow special. The word was a favourite of Adam's because of the ambiguity it held, teetering between euphemism and praise, and it became the title of a show in 1997. Kevin still remembered the day – not of the show, but of the sweets. It was the kind of story told often enough to have been burnished beyond recognition. Kevin wondered aloud where the picture might have ended up.

"Each wrapper was different. Each wrapper had a different colour. And he sat here all day, drawing them. That's when his mother recognised this kid was different," Kevin said. "I always understood him, but his mother had a deeper relationship with him. She was more spiritual than I, and Adam was very religious. He didn't let people know, but he was always aware of the presence of God. There was an uncertainty with his relationship with his mother. He felt it was inconsistent, but it wasn't. It was just that he would look for approval and she wouldn't give him the answer that he wanted."

When Adam and Kevin bonded, it was in the bush. At holidays, they would camp with family around Baradine or

Coonabarabran. The bush became Adam's obsession. His father's mastery of it was always his own shortcoming. But he loved the bush, and this made him love his father more.

"Adam loved to shoot. He was a shocking shot. He couldn't hit a bull's arse with a shotgun. And he didn't know what he was hitting," Kevin said. "He was a shocking rider, too. You saw him riding in at the Cullen Hotel on the white horse: Christ, he looked uncomfortable. With things like that he was very uncomfortable, and he knew the whole Cullen family is very adept at it. He looked up to my relationship with the bush, my connection to the bush and my relationship with my brothers, which he couldn't share with Mark. He wanted to have family so much."

*

Adam hunts through a ratty manila folder. I have seen it before: it holds the photograph of the tent in which his mother was born and pictures of relatives standing in forest camps, each with the same rounded jaw he inherited from her line. Adam is looking for a picture of his father but settles for a photograph of the Baradine windmills where his uncles worked. One of them lost an eye on the job, he says. He wears a patch and looks like a bad character actor.

"My grandparents, they owned the seventh house in Narromine. My father remembers as a real little kid hopping on the back of his dad's horse and going and watching corroborees," he says. "My parents, their hearts were in the bush."

Adam tried hard to find the bush in Collaroy's gums and paperbarks, in the suburban inflections of bougainvillea and cocos palms. But he never really succeeded. "Our place is not that far from the lakes. After school or on the weekends I would just go camping up the street," he says. "All of that bush joins onto the Ku-ring-gai National Park. We'd go canoeing, shooting with my guns. I had fun. Everything was just fun. I had fucking motorcycles. It was great. And I used to work with my father as a labourer. He was a builder and he paid real well: $100 a week as a teenager. I'd scour the *Trading Post* for guns and bikes. I was a member of the swimming club and the surf club. Australia is fucking paradise as far as I'm concerned. This planet is a miracle and we're fucking it up."

*

Kevin was proud when kids started calling him Young Mouse. He would carry his brother's bag to school and do his washing up in exchange for rides on his motorcycle. "I idolised Mouse. He was a mad rooter, but ladies loved him," Kevin said. "He was a good-looking fellow. He had an incredible reputation. Mouse didn't care whether they were married or not. If they were old enough to do it, or young enough to do it, Mouse was in like Flynn."

Mouse read electricity meters in Narromine and made a habit of sleeping with housewives, either in passion or to settle bills. He didn't mind either way, Kevin said. Narromine was a shearers' town and he made the most of work that kept men away from their wives until the sheds cut out. But even if their husbands were home, Mouse was game. His front amazed Kevin. "Her husband was just there," he said through fits of laughter. "And Mouse had her pants to the side and his finger in her snatch." A girl would come to stay next door, Kevin said, and Mouse would be around the same afternoon. "He was having a knee-trembler against the wall. My brother Frank and I couldn't stop laughing."

*

Kevin met his first wife, Elma Wilkie, at high school. "She was a pretty girl," he said, "but not small." They married in 1955 or 1956, Kevin cannot remember. "We didn't live happily ever after. The marriage lasted four years and she died of melanoma very quickly. The melanoma spread to her spinal cord, to her breasts. I was there when she died, which was pretty hard. I lost it a bit. When Adam died, I lost it a bit. I didn't want to do anything. The garden's a fucking shambles, but I'm coming back slowly."

Kevin mentioned again the woman who sold him eggs. He said the path she started him on was one he could not get off. It was furrowed by a lifetime of flirting, by a winking charm that was Kevin's most constant state – a talent for women that Adam said made him feel inadequate.

"I don't know whether she was a widow or her husband was a shearer," Kevin said, "but it was as often as I wanted it – every time I went to get eggs. At that age you're randy all the time. There was no dick sucking at that time. It was missionary or it wasn't. I remember she said, 'Kevin, all you've got to do is hang on. I'll do all the work.'"

Eventually, his mother twigged. He had become too enthusiastic for the chore and was asking too often if she needed eggs. "That was it. She started making me walk all the way to Mrs Weir. She was a Scot, and filthy."

*

Carmel was at a book launch when Kevin first saw her. He was there to drink, she was a sales girl from Farmer's. Kevin was several beers in by the time he decided he would talk to her. If Adam's relationship with his mother was complex, Kevin's was mostly simple. "Carmel was there in a red dress, in chiffon, with black hair – all of it. God, she was attractive." He spent the evening following her around and eventually convinced her to let him drive her home in the blue Vauxhall Velox ute that was his proudest possession at the time.

"We went home, we got inside. She's got asthma and she's taking the atomizer." Kevin quickens the story: "And she said 'Quick, Kevin. Undo my bra.' I could do this single-handed. Now, she's not a small woman and these bosoms just exploded out. I went in the next day to Farmer's book department to see covertly what she looked like in the daylight, and it was pretty good so I went up to her and that's how we started going out."

*

Adam had exhibited a few times before Kevin could no longer take the broken toys and calamine-painted mice he was showing. These early works were the vestiges of childhood, of summer holidays tinged with the menace of an adulthood Adam never wanted.

Kevin accepted immediately that Adam was an artist: that he did not want to do anything else, that he couldn't. But Kevin and Carmel both struggled with the talented high-school painter who was choosing instead to exhibit refuse. "We used to go to his exhibitions reluctantly, to see this junk stuff," Kevin said. "We were there as good parents. I couldn't stand it any longer and I said, 'Mate, who buys this shit?' Later, when he sold out a show, he looked at me and said, 'Da, these people buy this shit.'"

Yet Kevin was enormously proud of Adam's career, more so than Carmel. The more successful Adam became, the closer he became to his father. "His temperament didn't change, but the man did," Kevin said. "The art did, but the temperament didn't. Our relationship didn't. I'm sure we were the stability in his life, because we didn't change. We were always the same. Adam could put out his hand anytime and we would be there, the same people. All the art he did, he tried to shock you – bums and dicks and vahinas. But the more people looked at it, the more considered his art became."

*

Just before his second marriage, Adam's half-brother Mark moved home with his fiancée, an exotic dancer named Katie. "Very exotic, if you know what I mean," Kevin said. "She had a nice pair of tits, too. And I never saw her with a bra on."

A photograph of her sitting on Kevin's lap is part of family lore. It was reimagined by Adam in the 2004 painting *Artist and stepdaughter.* The picture shows Adam in a chair, a Medusa-haired woman straddling him in naked coition. She is buxom and remote; he is bald and hateful. It is not well painted, but the anger is obvious.

The issue surfaced three years earlier, in the painting *She must have known.* Adam had sketched out the work that most fascinated him as a boy, Goya's *Saturn Devouring His Son.* It was the Black Painting he had sat in front of as a child at the Prado, and he kept a postcard of the picture pinned to a wall at home. In Adam's rendition, Saturn's filicide is made sexual by the addition of a stumpy penis and a naked woman painted beside him, her mouth stitched and her genitals gaping. The title, Adam said, was directed at his mother: "Of course she fucking knew."

In the family photograph, Katie is wearing her wedding dress. She and Mark had married a few hours earlier. Katie has a glass of wine in one hand and blonde ringlets pinned around her face. Kevin is wearing a tuxedo with a red rose pinned to his lapel. He has one hand on her hip and she has a lace-sleeved arm draped around his shoulders. Both their faces are caught in ecstasy, laughing as Kevin pours a glass of red with his free hand.

"They lived upstairs in the flat I put on for them. They lived there for a year," Kevin says. "The marriage broke up and Katie lived a few streets away. Mark stayed up in the flat. Carmel said, 'You think you're welcoming her into the family, but she thinks you're having an affair.'"

Kevin is smiling his marsupial smile. "What did Bill Clinton say? 'I did not have sex with that woman.'" He winks at me. "But I copped the blame."

Kevin pulls out the photograph. It is in a box with pictures of his brothers and of Adam as a little boy, dressed as a cowboy or standing grinning and blond in front of various suburban fences. Kevin looks for a second at himself and then at Katie and he smiles. "Do I love my life in that picture?"

*

Adam was a boy by the time Kevin heard Carmel sing for the first time. It was at a cousin's wedding and Adam had become fractious during the ceremony. Kevin took him outside to draw fish in the sand. "Carmel started to sing, and it was so beautiful Adam started to cry and so did I," he said. "'Ave Maria' can rip your heart out, especially when it is sung like that."

While Adam was uncomfortable with Carmel's career, Kevin revelled in it. The house is hung with promotional material, and the top room is stacked with tapes of her television appearances. Adam's high-school paintings are on one wall and the poster from her Hungry Jacks commercial is on another. "She could hit high C," Kevin says. "Who do you know who could hit high C? She didn't get to the Opera House, but she was a trained opera singer."

*

Mark sat behind Kevin at Adam's funeral, but the two men did not talk. Kevin believes Mark was jealous of Adam's success, and says his resentment drove a wedge between them. They see each other only at funerals. "He could be dead for all I know," Kevin says. "He was at Carmel's funeral. I didn't speak to him. He didn't want to speak to me, didn't want to speak to Adam."

Kevin did not speak to Mark, but he did speak to Katie. He saw her once more, after Carmel died. "Katie came back," he says. "She knew Carmel had died and she came back here."

But Kevin no longer trusted her intentions. He was made nervous by her phone call and refused to let her into the house. They talked on the threshold. "How lucky am I?" he says. "I would have fucked her and it would have been the dumbest thing I had done. But I didn't let her in – I gave her a hundred dollars and called a cab."

*

Adam talked more about his mother than his father. He felt he had more to settle with her. But his father was the greater influence. In some respects, it was his father's machismo that crippled him. "He's a real man, you know? Actually a real fucking man," Adam said. "Da is my hero. He can do anything. But I'm not actually that much like him. I'd like to be, but I'm not. I suppose he will always just be there, and it makes me aware of what I'm not, that he's this man – this real man – and I'm fucking pretending."

Love was difficult for Adam, but he loved his father unconditionally. "I don't think he was envious," Kevin said, referring to his own bush childhood. "He was always aware it was a past era, and he would try to emulate parts of it."

The influence Kevin had on Adam never worried him. He was as pragmatic about fathering as he was about building. "I never thought about it. I was unaware of the effect I was having on him. It was the power of example. Kids need a father figure, and the fact I was an energetic dad was always there. The influence on Adam, the influence I had, was just being there. I was his example, and in a crude sense we did 'stuff'. I could swim as good as him. I could run faster than him. I could tell lies as well as him. And he got all of that from me. If I just sat there and watched television, he would have been sick to death of me and he would have got bored, but he didn't. We were always together."

Adam told me, just before he died, that he could not bear the thought of outliving his father.

*

"Flirting, I just can't help it," Kevin says. "Adam would never get a root unaided. He had to have some help: a suit or something. With me, I'm from nine to ninety. I went to a funeral a couple of years ago: there was an old sheila, she cracked onto me, holding on to me here and here and here."

Stories pour out of Kevin: Carmel spilling tea over a secretary he fancied, with thighs as wide as his waist; young girls who still compliment him on his clothes; the neighbour he flirts with on her birthday. "Her husband doesn't fix her up properly, and one year I called her up and gave her a dirty phone call: 'I'm going to take your panties off, I'm going to fuck you.' Nothing too serious, but she loved it," he says. "There is nothing worse than a woman who isn't fixed up properly, and I can't do everyone."

But Kevin insists he was always faithful. Adam's concerns were imagined. "Carmel never worried about me. She was like Paul Newman – 'It's alright to study the menu, as long as you eat at home.'" He pauses to meet my eye for the punchline: "But I could be a shocking flirt."

*

Kevin's mother, Sadie, stayed with the family for a month each summer, when Narromine became too hot, when the whole town became so scorched that the horizon evaporated and wooden buildings creaked as if they were alive. She was not easily impressed by Kevin's girlfriends; even when he was a boy she would complain the girls he brought home were too common. "Mum never liked Carmel," he said. "She thought she was a bad woman and never looked after her husband properly – but she looked after me like a fucking king."

In earshot of Carmel, his mother once asked another woman, "Why does he always marry fat women who drink? He does it all the time."

Kevin moved with Carmel to Collaroy six weeks after Adam was born. It was a difficult block, which Kevin had bought with his first wife. Everywhere are the accents of an owner-builder: a room of stucco walls, a solitary stained-glass window in the front, arches everywhere they will fit. It is a house that looks to have grown out of weekends, climbing up an open staircase, and then a twisting wooden one, until the roof itself is filled with rooms. "If you're bored," Kevin says, "put on a room."

The house fascinated Adam. It confirmed for him his belief that his father could do anything. In moments of self-doubt he would complain of art's uselessness by comparison: "My father builds houses with his bare fucking hands." The house held a kind of magic for Adam, as if it had sprouted from his childhood imagination. Adam's paintings had two major themes, innocence and suburbia, and this house was both.

"Adam was so aware as a kid," Kevin says. "Everything was new. He would embrace things with all of his senses. I think that Adam – the fact that he was able to move freely with his life, to observe, to listen, to make things up – I think that Adam felt secure. He wasn't restricted in anything he did. He knew that Carmel and I were a loving couple in every way. He never feared that she and I wouldn't be together in this house forever."

*

The lie began in Adam's master's thesis, the myth that a painting had started his stutter. "I was painting and drawing at an early age. I was drawing before I could talk," he wrote. "I was very young when in Spain I spent hours staring up at Goya's 'Saturn Devouring His Son'. On arriving at Sydney airport I started to stutter – this lasted a few years until I got it under control."

The story was repeated in the catalogue essay for *Blindside,* a travelling show in 1999. Eventually, it made it into his newspaper obituaries. As so often with Adam, the lie became fact.

"That was the beginning of the revolution for we three," Kevin said of the two months the family spent in Spain in 1975. "We didn't realise at the time what an effect it was having on Adam. I had always wanted to go to Spain. If I didn't marry Carm, I would have gone away and not come back. I was interested in the flamenco guitar and I wanted to learn it in Spain. I hear Spanish music and it's just magnificent. It gets to my soul. As a kid from Narromine, I just knew I had to get to Spain."

The trip also took them through Italy. A solicitor cousin of Carmel's had bungled her first divorce, and she was worried she might be charged with bigamy after marrying Kevin. "I was anxious to get an annulment so we could be married," she said. "We were blessed by everyone else but the Pope and it was brilliant: we were free."

At the Prado, Carmel noticed something change in Adam. He became quiet, more focused. He spent hours in the Goya room, sitting on the parquetry floor and looking up at the pictures. "From that moment, that was the start of something big," she said. "We were there two or three days. But Adam – the thing that fascinated him about Goya was that he had twenty children. Adam sat up and said, 'He must have mated twenty times.' He said that in the middle of the museum."

Adam was already stuttering when he went to Spain. It had begun a year before the trip. His stutter frustrated him, but he liked the fact he shared it with his father. "I understood exactly what he was going through," Kevin said. "I was a stutterer myself. I started at twelve and it lasted until I was twenty. I hated it. I must have sounded like an idiot." Kevin's stutter was controlled, but Adam's persisted. Words would catch on his teeth when he was angry or nervous. He seemed pained by the hesitation, by the pause between sentences as he tried to force out the next word with his tongue. "It's incredibly frustrating," Adam said. "You're trying to express yourself and it's just not enough."

Goya did not cause the stutter. More likely, Adam's father did. "It could have been Kevin," Carmel said. "He was so go, go, go and Adam just couldn't get things out fast enough, and he would just get him so excited."

When Adam was a child, Kevin made a habit of leaving the house in various states of absurdity. Even now, at seventy-eight, he sometimes fetches the morning paper in a dress. While Adam was having breakfast, Kevin would leave for work without pants: his trousers would be hidden in his briefcase to put on later, but he would exit the house naked from the waist down, nothing between his shirt tails and his sock garters. Other times, he would have a tie on but no shirt. "Adam would be beside himself," Kevin said. "That might be where it started. He was so desperate to tell me what was wrong."

Adam confessed eventually that the story about the cause of his stuttering was make-believe. He would stick to a lie, but only for so long. He thought Goya made a better anecdote than his father's pranks. "I think it came from just not knowing what was happening," he said. "I suppose I have always had an incredible imagination. I was always an outsider at home. I just think there was this other world. If I had to talk quickly or answer, I had to think of other words. It actually increased my fucking vocabulary."

*

Adam blamed Kevin for nothing. He felt envious sometimes, or inadequate, but never judgemental. Both were extraordinarily forgiving of each other. It was Kevin who dealt with the police when Adam stole a buggy from the Cromer Golf Club. He was unfazed by the stupidity of teenage boys. "It was just a non-event, really," Kevin said of the sergeant. "He treated us like the local bloody country policeman. There was no blood. They didn't throw him into the can."

Kevin dealt with the school when Adam rode his motorbike into the teachers' common room, when he was in trouble for running out on lessons or fighting in the playground. Even when Adam was a child, Kevin was his greatest defender.

"It was typical Adam stuff: it challenges without being crude," he said. "He left here because he was bored with us. He said, 'Mum, I love you dearly, but I can't make art here. There's too much love here for me, so I'm going where the action is. I'm going nowhere here.'

"We let him go. We couldn't hold him back anyway because he was too big. He moved bloody everywhere. He really did. He was a complete bloody bum, but I think that was necessary. I don't want to give him too much credit, but he was getting himself through an initiation of fire. He nearly killed himself, but we didn't want to know about that. There's a lot of stuff I don't want to know about."

SEX

"It's alright. I'm not going to fuck you."

There is nothing dramatic about Adam's black eye. He fell on the back stairs, shifting pot plants in the rain. But the swelling makes it difficult to cry. The tears pool in the purpled flesh and the bruises make painful his attempts to wipe them away.

"You probably know I'm on the border of bisexual," Adam says through the crying. "I think you can smell me a mile away."

We are sitting in the front room of his house. The lights are off. A newly acquired bearskin lies in front of us, the head still attached. An enormous fish trap has arrived since I was last here. This is among the only interviews we have done without drink or drugs. His court case for weapons possession ended only a few weeks earlier. Adam says he is ashamed: in public, he has only ever been straight.

"I prefer the company of men," Adam offers, "as a lot of writers and artists have said." He pushes through the tears, fending off emotion as if giving some urgent instructions. He knows he will soon change the subject, but he wants to finish this thought. "Women – and this is a great quote – my father said that the best advice his father gave him – my grandfather, Fred, who I haven't met – he said,

'Kevin, be careful: women are queer cattle.'" Adam had used a similar line when we first met: "As my granddaddy said, 'If it's got tits, wheels or fur, you're fucked.'"

Adam stops trying to wipe away the tears. He cries openly and his speech becomes unvarnished. But he looks away to make his points. I have rarely seen him so uncomfortable.

"I haven't been openly gay or bi before, but I prefer men because women are fucking stupid," he says. "I do like holding men. Holding men is nice. We people are great specimens. I suppose I should quote Shakespeare: 'What a piece of work is a man.'"

Classroom *Hamlet* is perhaps the right place to start: Adam was at school when he first realised he liked men, although he immediately suppressed the feeling. He had not really had girlfriends. Women were scared of him. He blamed his stutter but didn't understand it.

*

The first night I stay at Adam's place in Wentworth Falls, the little cottage is quilted by fog. These are the first and coldest days of winter. The air is wet with cloud. Cold freezes trees against the sky, jack-frosting their branches as in a velvet painting. All day the valley has been filling up with mist until eventually it spills over and swallows the house itself.

Adam has shot up on the couch, where we are sitting side by side. The conversation is about his mother. He is working at extending a track mark that is gradually underlining the shamrock tattoo on his forearm, as if the clover leaf is a scout badge inexpertly stitched to him. We have been drinking vodka from tin mugs, gunky where the price had been stuck to them in whichever camping store they were bought.

"You need to shower," Adam says to me. "I want you to shower for me." His eyes are rolling in and out of opiate blinks. He sways a little. Adam leans his body against mine, although I am not sure if the gesture is sexual. He is both affectionate and aggressive. His whole presence is heavy. "I want you to shower."

Poor circulation gives Adam's fingertips a bluish tinge, which makes more of the pink crescents where he has chewed his nails down past the quick. It also highlights the scratches that take forever to heal. He pushes his hand onto my leg and squeezes my thigh until it starts to hurt. Heroin has slowed his speech. Everything seems to be moving more slowly. His hand moves up and down my leg, resting occasionally to grip my thigh. He mutters the word "good" over and over. I don't know how to move.

After a long silence Adam gets up and walks to another room. I can hear him looking for something, pulling books off shelves. He comes back with a folded towel and a cake of motel soap. Its wrapping is waxy and crinkled from coming in and out of bags.

He asks me again to shower and I make a series of excuses. He pleads with me. What started as a demand now sounds like a desperate entreaty. "Just shower," he says. "Please."

*

At school Adam liked mixing with the strong boys. "I was always the outsider. I was in with the bad group, but the smartest of the bad group. I was in English 1 and Art 1 and they were in English 4. Most of my friends lived in fibros."

He had a girlfriend in his final year. They got drunk together at school camp – he remembered her being impressed that he had brought alcohol – but nothing sexual occurred between them. He was nervous around her and sensed she was scared of him. Fear is a constant in the way he talks about sex – why it happens and why it doesn't. Life to Adam is an unending assessment of who can handle him and who cannot.

It was at art school that Adam lost his virginity, later than his friends. "Art school was basically a sex fest – no boys, but as I get older I enjoy the company of men," he says. "Men can handle me now. They used to be scared of me. Men are straight shooters, as a hunter would say."

By the time we talk about his sexuality, Adam is reading William S. Burroughs obsessively, especially the gay novella *Queer*. He is excited by the thought that Burroughs shot his wife and boasts that he attacked his own long-term partner, Carrie, with a cattle prod. The truth is he threatened her with a knife and a gun. An apprehended violence order against him was granted shortly afterwards.

"I have thought about sleeping with men, but it's nothing more than hugs. It's a little bit like Bill Burroughs. A lot of bisexual men like hugs. I just like hugging men. Women can't do that – they're fucking weak at it. You can't hold a woman."

I think of an ink and collage work Adam made in 1996, called *I like the suburbs*. He was interested at the time in manifestos. In the work, alongside campaign stickers for the Truck Safe Foundation and a scrapbook doodle, he wrote one for himself:

> I've always lived in the northern suburbs
> I like the suburbs
> There's no wogs
> No gooks
> No blacks
> This is why I really like
> Blowing up letter boxes
> With copper pipe bombs
> When I'm bored I watch
> The girls next door
> Play with their things
> And I wonder why I'm here

All the time dying
I'm really happy
But not gay
One bit.

*

During that first week staying in Adam's spare room, I twice woke to find him standing over my bed. There was a shotgun propped in one corner and a crossbow in another. A signed poster of the Wenham portrait was framed on one wall, like a piece of pool-room memorabilia. Beside the bed was an anonymous puddle of dried vomit, puckering the carpet into rough peaks. The sheets were silk and yellowed, darkened where other bodies had lain. The bed had a gathered skirt that seemed faintly ridiculous, as though a teenage boy were living in his grandmother's house.

The windows were always shuttered, but in the darkness it was clear Adam was naked. He would stand there for a moment, neither of us saying anything, and then he would leave. There was nothing menacing about his presence. He seemed nervous. Drugs had made his body insubstantial. The morning after this first happened he told me a long and contradictory story about how he suffered as a sleepwalker.

*

"Handsome" was Adam's greatest term of affection. Paintings were never beautiful, certainly not pretty: they were handsome. He coined the term "hetero-camp" to describe what he liked about the glamour of a bullfight: the *traje de luces*, the suit of lights. They reminded him of his own performance art. In Barcelona on an artist residency, he had watched six bullfights a day and produced almost no work.

Violence and sex for him were always intertwined. At art school, his aesthetic was forged from the danger of both. He dressed like a skinhead and described as "savage" his relationship with campus feminists. He boasted that he had been a member of the ultra-right National Front and part of a gang that had kicked to death a gay man. "I never really conformed with the group," he said. "I hung around with the skinheads because I liked the skinheads. I wasn't necessarily a Nazi, but I have always been interested in the existence of the extreme right. It's just so handsome. I used to love to go and see bands that would attract that crowd."

He claimed to have played trumpet briefly and poorly with the punk band feedtime, and with another called Lubricated Goat. This was, so far as I could tell, untrue. "I used to love clothes, really nice skinhead clothes," he said. "I could never get hassled by anyone. Nice shoes. Skinny braces, fucking white ones. Of course, I got called a poof when I studied art. But not regularly."

*

Adam steers through the Blue Mountains in the Holden FC he loved but was mostly prevented by court order from driving. It is the cold autumn of 2010. He is talking about us checking into a hotel together. This is a recurrent request, plaintive and sometimes frantic. He is like a schoolboy planning a sleepover. "Just a night," he says. "It will be great. You and me, getting away. We'll check into a nice bed and breakfast. It will just be a night."

We end up camped on a verge in the Megalong Valley. Adam tries and fails to kindle a fire. "Sometimes I feel so weak I just sit there and cry," he says. "I think I'm kind of done with tenderness. I'm not looking for a relationship unless I sort of fall sideways into one. But I think I need to set up in a new town with new people. Sometimes I'm just so lonely, you know?"

The next morning, I find Adam unconscious in his sleeping bag. He is covered in his own vomit. It is the beginning of an episode of diabetic ketoacidosis that will see him spend a week in Katoomba Hospital. He is put in the room in which his uncle died two years earlier.

*

Resentment courses through everything Adam says. He is shaking now as he works through a list of girlfriends. Carrie Lumby is the first he mentions, although she was not his first. They met at a gallery opening in 1993 and began a decade-long relationship that coincided with the most productive years of his career. Adam said she suspected his interest in men. "I think Carrie had her suspicions, but I was never unfaithful. Women are horny all the time, but I'm just not – I'm not horny. Girls lie. They think they're God's gift. If they didn't have a cunt, they would be stacked eight foot high at the tip. They are weak. I'm not. I'm not fucking weak."

It is early evening and a truck has just collected the portrait of Gareth Samson that will hang in the Archibald Prize. Adam is drunk and a little strung out. "I am a very lonely person," he says. "But I'm happy. People are basically stupid, so I can't have a real conversation. But then there's this other thing called physical intimacy I miss. I miss that closeness."

He returns to Lumby: "She was an alcoholic. She was here and she didn't pay for anything. I was actually her career. She was a complete nightmare and she drove me to drink heavily just to cope. She had me driving down to the grog shop four times a day."

And then to Cash Brown, his final girlfriend, also an artist: "Cash – that really hurt, looking back and realising that I've been left. She was just scared. She always said I'm much too dangerous to be around, emotionally and physically. She once said that because we have a good time, she's a good friend. I could never hate her. She's into everything I'm into. If you can imagine a female version of me – if you can imagine it, that's her. She just thought, this guy's on his way to hell and I don't really want to see him there. She didn't really want to go there with me. I'm still angry, but I could never hate the girl. She's really hardcore. It's hard – and this is a quote – it's hard to find a good hard girl."

Adam says Brown wrote to his father when the relationship ended, concerned about his drug habit and his drinking. The letter, to Adam's mind, was a great betrayal. "Maybe I was expecting too much, but I don't have an emotional or relationship barrier. You either ask too much or too little. That's why I live alone, because people just ask for too much."

Transcribing this from the shorthand in my notepad, I am reminded of something Carrie told me in the one interview we did after Adam died. It reminded me of Adam's relationship with his mother, too. Carrie was a strong woman, like Cash. Both had the toughness Adam required from relationships. "What he hated about women," Carrie said, "is that he needed them."

*

As soon as I arrive, Adam tells me the police are coming. He is not clear on what the crime is, but he says Carrie has called them. He hands me packing tape and kangaroo skins and tells me to help wrap his collection of firearms. The plan is to hide them inside the wall of his back shed, behind a painting of Max Cullen he did for the Moran Prize.

"She's actually the devil," he says as we work to wrap the weapons. "She's a tough. She's a liar. She's bad news. She thinks she's a really good person, which I think is a good sign of a really bad one."

The police never come. The episode was entirely imagined. A week later Adam calls and accuses me of stealing his guns. I tell him they are in the wall cavity. He hangs up after telling me not to take him for a fool.

*

"I give people their best, but then they screw me up," Adam says. "Have some guts or some balls or some honesty. Everything I have is on the table. You don't fuck with me. I'm happy single. I'm sick of people. I mean, I act badly, but I don't hurt people. I only hurt myself." He turns the conversation to loneliness, which will become a regular theme of these soliloquies. "It's not hurtful anymore," he says. "It's just disappointing. I'm just over these people."

We are in the studio, after Adam has been released from hospital. He is high. A temporary stent has been inserted to contain his leaking bile, but his skin has a sickly yellow afterglow. "I sort of wish Cash Brown loved me as much as I loved her," he says. "I think she was always a little bit scared of me. I think that's what love's about – being scared."

*

Adam was an obsessive. He would fixate on people. Phone calls would come at any hour. Emails would arrive in my inbox in volleys, no time allowed for a response. Their punctuation was as erratic as their thoughts. "Hello mate ..have you been stolen away, like a beautiful child ??" began one. "...must see you ...lots to talk within ! ..? call me mate ..ive got time at moment ..two shows approaching".

Seconds later, in an email titled "Please call me": "HEY DIG ... CALL ME YEA ! ADXOO" And then again: "CALL ME DIGGER. ADXOO". And then the next one, titled "Are you dead": "Are you ok??.please call ..i miss you .. adxo".

Sometimes these messages would come from nowhere, about conversations never had: "Hey dig, great to hear ya voice''..talk real soon .. u r' the last intell'' bloke in the world!!!! I need a real big hug ! ///telling me every things god dammn ok !@..yours always .. ad';' xoo".

Or plans unmade: "I WISH I WAS WITH YOU , I MISS YOU ...ANYWAY , WE SHOULD GO AWAY TOGETHER ...MAY BE ASIA SOME WHERE WEIRD !! ... LOVE , AD'' XXOO".

Sometimes they were lonely, empty but for the sign-off: "love you, Ad xxoo".

In email, Adam was never guarded: "i need you !! ..ad''x".

*

We are in Adam's studio, talking about his mother. He says, again, that she neglected his feelings. Immediately, he is talking about sex. "Women are great, but they should be avoided as much as possible. What's the point? Ten seconds of exalted pleasure? What's the fucking point? Women are like polar bears: beautiful at a distance, but stay away from them. They will kill you. They will eat you. I've been celibate for eighteen months. There's nothing like a skinny chick in bed, but you never want them to wake up in the morning. I'm not sure that can be seen as misogyny, because it's not."

It would be another year before Adam and I first talked about his sexuality, but the subject is scratching at the edges of our conversation. "I have come to a point where I'm a little bit confused. Not with myself – I'm always fine – but with other people. The more I avoid women, the happier I feel. That's odd. I don't know what it means, but it's great. It's leaving my head very empty and I can fill it with other things."

*

I ask Adam why he has hidden from his sexuality, but he doesn't have an answer. He has only just announced these feelings. I suspect it is because, at heart, he wants badly to be a country boy – to be some copy of his father: charming, funny, good with women. Instead, he has created for himself a character of violent machismo that would have been destroyed by his affection for men.

I had been incurious about Adam's sexuality. Certainly, I had been incurious about him romantically and I had never properly considered our relationship. Suddenly, it is all there: the showers, the nudity, the elegiac emails, the lingering touches, the fantasies about taking hotel rooms together, the pretense of this book with which he has convinced me to stay at his house. I think back to something Adam said early in our interviews, a line I never really understood: "You're the only man for me." Sitting opposite him, I finally twig: Adam is in love with me.

I ask if this hidden sexuality is the reason he has worked so hard to distance himself from society, the reason he has become so isolated and so resentful of the world. "It's some of it," he says. "It's a fucking lot of it, actually."

At the end of the interview, Adam pauses in the stunted hallway between me and the front door. He opens his arms to be hugged. Adam presses his body against mine, squeezing my torso as hard as he can. His eyes close, one black and the other now red from crying. The grip is so firm it hurts. Breath is forced from my lungs.

"It's alright," he whispers in my ear. "I'm not going to fuck you."

COURT

"I was rather fucking worried."

Adam meets me for a cigarette at the coffee shop in front of the Downing Centre – the old Mark Foy's building in Sydney, once a department store, now a district courthouse. He is sitting at one table and Kevin is sitting at another with his new partner, Elizabeth, and an old girlfriend of Adam's. "Everyone's concerned at the severity of the whole thing," Adam says. "Except Kev has just been irrefutably upbeat. That might be a mechanism. It might be how he relates to it."

Adam's arm is in a sling. Two nights earlier he almost overdosed in his studio. After passing out, he woke to find his hand numb – the result of nerve damage more often related to major trauma but in this instance caused by the weight of his unconscious body on the limb. "They call it a waiter's tip palsy," he says. "Because my arm is tucked up like a fucking waiter waiting for a tip. It will be six months before I can use it again." He was in hospital the day before and almost missed the court appearance. Doctors sometimes call Adam's injury Saturday night palsy, because of its association with extreme intoxication. Today is Thursday.

"He was as scared as a cat," Kevin says while Adam sits alone and finishes another cigarette. "He came late, of course. He didn't want to drink anything. This morning he couldn't dress himself. He was just standing there in his underpants. Elizabeth had to come and take the shirt out of the packet and iron the thing and take the pins out and put his pants on. He wouldn't eat anything last night. He said he would just throw it up. He didn't eat anything again this morning."

Kevin is nervous. He is dressed in black, retelling old stories. "Adam said, 'I left home because it's too happy. I can't make art here. You don't fight. You don't swear. You don't throw beer cans over the fence.' He had to go where the action was. So much for stability. But he does have nice manners. We got him a motorbike. That's where it started. He rode the thing into the teacher's common room like a cowboy. That's where it started."

*

The police fact sheet begins with a gentle description of Adam's antecedents: "The accused is an artist, he is currently suffering from mild depression and diabetes."

Adam had just driven out of a service station at Crookwell when police stopped him. He smelt strongly of alcohol and blew positive on a breath test. When the officers asked him to get out of his car, he was unsteady on his feet and struggling to follow directions. But it was not until he was locked in the back of a paddy wagon that police found the store of guns in the Toyota Hilux he had traded in exchange for two motorcycles. There were three firearms on the back seat, ten more in the boot, a .357 calibre revolver tucked into a pocket behind the driver's seat. Ammunition was scattered through the car. A further search found a bag containing a slingshot, a taser and a pen gun Adam had made in Year Ten metalwork.

An ambulance was called twenty minutes after Adam was taken into custody. His blood sugars had become dangerously high. He refused to be taken to hospital. An hour and a half passed before his blood alcohol concentration was properly tested. He twice failed to blow sufficient air into the machine. On the third try, he returned a reading of 0.132 – almost three times the legal limit.

At this point, the fact sheet records, Adam asked a question: "Is that high?"

*

I notice Adam's belt buckle as we wait in line for the court security checks. It is an impressive oval stamped with the insignia of Smith & Wesson, the American arms manufacturer. It seems a peculiar choice at a weapons appearance. Adam had arrived wearing thongs and coloured socks but has since changed into the brass-capped larrikin heels he wore at his mother's funeral.

A thick-set security guard stops the conveyor belt that is feeding into the X-ray machine and holds up a duffle bag. It is Adam's. The guard opens it. There are loose sheets of Physeptone and needles for his diabetes. Pills have broken out of various containers and are strewn through the mess. The guard fishes around and finds an old set of shearer's cutters, like a pair of sharpened metal dentures.

The bag goes through the machine again. The guard talks to the man operating the conveyor belt. They look troubled. He digs through the bag and produces a twelve-inch hunting knife. Adam protests that he will want it back – it is a favourite, he says.

"You can pick it up at Surry Hills Police Station," the guard says. "Although you'll probably get arrested. You can't walk around on the street with that. It's illegal."

News of Adam's charges broke on the cover of the *Sydney Morning Herald* five days earlier. The headline said everything: "All I was doing was making art. I am very, very scared. I have never hurt anyone, ever." The piece quoted Edmund Capon in a character reference prepared for the court. Capon was Adam's great supporter, and he was careful to portray Adam as a thoughtful artist, not the reckless character he sometimes seemed:

> Adam Cullen's work is acute and often satirical; his imagery can be quite confronting but it is a powerful echo of so much of contemporary life. Most of all, Adam Cullen is a contemporary artist of great

seriousness and to truly pursue his art, he lives what some may see as a peripheral existence. That is often the role of the artist; to experience the extremes in order to incisively observe the commonplace.

*

There is a tea break. The matter is moved from one courtroom to another. The five blinking lifts that once heaved with hatted shoppers disgorge petty criminals into the waiting room. Downstairs, the foyer is dressed with the marble tiles and gilt trim of a department store. A great spiral staircase winds through the middle of it. Upstairs, bureaucracy has moved in. Signs tell people to wait at unattended desks. Some are laminated, some tattered paper. One cheerily announces a "Police Witness Meeting Area". Everything is mauve or blue or Laminex. Banks of formed-plastic chairs sit along walls. The criminal registry is confettied with deli chits, numbers given to the production line of people waiting for their court documents to be processed. Authority is set in wood panelling and frosted glass, undone by the ratty office chairs pushed behind the bar tables in each courtroom.

"We're just constructing a story out of little bits and pieces. It's just so opaque," Adam says during the break. "And we're just looking for the little connections and the bits I can't remember. It is aggravating. It's that weird space where the legal ones I had and the illegal ones I had – the illegal ones might have been inoperable, or I might have used them on the day. All these things go to constructing the story. Because I was scared, I suppose, I was very compliant and just acquiesced. I was rather fucking worried."

*

Standing in Court 4.7, Charles Waterstreet fumbles a little with the brief. He has been Adam's lawyer since the two met at one of Robert Hughes' mud-crab parties, although until now Adam's demands on him have been mostly trivial: occasional legal advice and representation for drink-driving offences. Waterstreet is straggle-haired and scoundrel-faced and wretchedly likeable. Adam calls him Chilla, after his uncle. He appears today in exchange for a portrait Adam painted of him, which hung in this year's Archibald Prize. "It's worth $25,000," Adam says.

Waterstreet wishes to run a Section 32 – dispensation for Adam to be dealt with under the *Mental Health (Forensic Provisions) Act* – but he does not have the treatment plan such an application would require. The magistrate notes this. Adam draws his fingers into the shape of a gun behind his back and while the magistrate speaks fires two imaginary bullets into the ground. No plea is entered. The case is set over for a month.

Outside, Waterstreet makes small talk with Kevin. "No finality today, but it will be fine," he says. "A bit of an anticlimax, but most of my dates are." And to Adam: "Life works like that. It will be fine."

*

The gallery assistant did not recognise Edmund Capon as he arrived – not his jesting, leathering, craggy-cheeked face; not his preternaturally blond hair or his deliberately mismatched socks. In the darkened gallery he looked every bit the Archibald portrait Adam had painted of him, his features seemingly made of dripping ice-cream, a Neapolitan grotesquery. Capon was early for the opening of Adam's show at Chalkhorse Gallery, held two months before the court appearance that arose from its production. When Adam was arrested in Crookwell, he was driving back from a few days spent making work for the show, titled *Independent Judiciary (Mother's Milk).*

The premise of the show was reasonably basic: Adam would paint targets on canvases and line up paint pots and spray cans in front of them, then shoot at the vessels until sufficient colour had been splattered against the picture behind. The results, however, were at once sensitive and comic. Punctured spray cans spun over the pictures like Catherine wheels. The torn canvas looked strangely medical. Pride and stupidity brimmed in the biro arrows Adam drew to mark where he had hit the tiny sheets of paper he was also showing. There was a forlorn meaninglessness, a sense of self-mockery. The acting out, as ever, related to childhood. The responsibility was always his parents'. "I lost my Mummy. 14 July 2010," he spray-painted onto a canvas called *Ain't no game like a fox.*

In a catalogue essay, Oliver Watts rightly saw these as a return to the grunge work Adam made early in his career. He noted the anxiety and the yearning. As Adam's charges awaited a court, Watts also began the construction of a defence:

> Shooting at a canvas is by its very nature impotent; there is no external target or result merely a feedback loop, a ricochet. The work is not violently and passionately made but safely: they are done on private property; with legal weapons; in a creative not destructive act.

Chalkhorse is a tiny space in what was once the loading dock of a warehouse complex. Adam had not shown in spaces like this for more than a decade. Watts came out of one of the artist studios in the complex just as Capon was leaving. He apologised but said Adam was not there.

It was the last time Cullen might have seen his great supporter. Unknown to Watts or Capon, he was slumped in a studio, smoking a cigarette and trying to balance his insulin levels. "It's a shame. A fucking big shame," Adam said later. "But he came. That's good, isn't it?"

*

The fact sheet continues. Adam told police he ate a single chicken leg while drinking a "middy of liqueur" – later described as a bottle of vodka mixed with cranberry juice and Coca-Cola.

Police juggled a video camera as they searched Adam's car. The roll call of weapons was almost humorous, such was its length: a Wesson Arms .357 revolver, registered to an owner in the ACT; an unregistered .22 rifle, make unknown; a US Carbine M1 .30 self-loading rifle, also unregistered; an unregistered .410 shotgun; an unregistered Ruger .22 self-loading rifle; two antique muzzle-loaded firearms; seven more firearms registered to Adam. Tallied up, there were six charges: one for drink-driving, two for possessing a prohibited weapon without a permit, two for possessing unregistered firearms, one for possessing an unauthorised pistol.

Given the seriousness of the offences, Adam was transferred from Crookwell Police Station to Goulburn. At 10.15 pm, five hours after he was stopped by police, he submitted to an interview. The conversation was never transcribed. In it, he admitted he used the guns, although only to make art. The slingshot, he said, was for shooting letterboxes.

Adam calls me two days later, having just made bail. “You need to write me a character reference,” he says. “You’re an important person. This court needs to realise how fucking powerful I am.”

*

The day of the hearing finally arrives. Adam talks to Waterstreet outside the courtroom, by now more interested in the press than the charges. “The *Australian* is here,” he says. “And the *Tele.* And the *Herald.*” Waterstreet goes to speak with an associate. Adam holds my arm: “I’ve just never really been so confused about anything really. I can feel it getting closer, but I just don’t know how it will go.”

The magistrate is a neat blonde woman. She has the dry speaking voice of a nice person attempting to seem severe. A few months earlier she had written herself into the newspapers when she cleared a court, complaining that the smell of rodents in her chambers had become unbearable. “If it’s not the air-conditioning breaking down,” she said at the time, “it’s rats dying and being left to rot.” The five minutes of silence as she reads the brief are excruciating, but she breaks them warmly: “Are you pursuing a Section 32?”

Waterstreet steps forward. Adam is sitting alone, strapping and unstrapping the velcro on his splinted arm – the palsy from last month’s court appearance showing no sign of healing. Kevin is sitting behind him, dressed in the same black fedora and suit he was wearing here four weeks earlier. Beside me, a man with neck tattoos and an amphetamine gauntness flicks through images on his phone. He is waiting to be called on a petty theft charge.

"This is a coalescence of symptoms where my client has come to an intersection in his life where his very life is at peril," Waterstreet says. "This day was a day where he was going to create, I'll say, a legitimate work of art." The man with neck tattoos sits forward. His girlfriend stops fidgeting with her bracelets. Waterstreet continues: "The vodka he drank was in aid of some misguided artistic inspiration." The man with neck tattoos laughs a muffled laugh I assume he has been laughing from the back of rooms since primary school.

"He was a collector of firearms, obviously," Waterstreet goes on, ignoring the laugh. "He had them for curiosity value." More laughter. "He is the registered owner of eight firearms." The gaunt man stops laughing, his eyes widening at the childlike absurdity of the charges Waterstreet is walking us through. "He no longer has the slingshot."

Adam straps and unstraps his splint. The magistrate interrupts: "Why would I deal with this under the mental health provision rather than law? I just can't see that." Waterstreet pleads that Adam is perilously ill. He takes eleven medications a day. He was recently diagnosed as bipolar. Diabetes sees him frequently in hospital. "His alcohol problems have been taken over by physical events, and he's had his pancreas removed."

It is as if Waterstreet is flailing around in a hospital file looking for a defence. He has the imp's capacity to make even a rehearsed statement seem dishevelled. The charges sit there while illnesses pile up around them. The magistrate interrupts again, perhaps to help the barrister away from himself. In reality, he has already done his job. "I won't," she says, "be sending him to jail."

*

In the months between being arrested and facing court, Adam became obsessed with amassing character references. It was a task with which he could distract himself. By the end, there were too many to table. There were references from his art dealers, from the wife of Chopper Read, from the chief photographer at the *Weekend Australian Magazine*, from the deputy mayor of Upper Lachlan Council, on whose property Adam had been shooting before he was arrested. A director of the Humane Society International wrote to take partial responsibility for the charges, having suggested Adam produce work with a "dodging bullets" theme for an upcoming charity auction. "I can't help but feel slightly responsible," Verna Simpson wrote, "for Adam having firearms in his car."

One reference arrived from a former attorney-general, Duncan Kerr, who was in Papua New Guinea when Adam contacted him, working on a constitutional challenge to Sir

Michael Somare's ouster as prime minister. It began by apologising for the fact that, as he was in Port Moresby, the correspondence was without his chamber's letterhead. He continued:

> I am aware that Adam Cullen can be rash, is provocative and can be disturbingly ugly in his depictions of his subject matter – particularly when he confronts things we wish not to see. I know some of his work teeters along the thin edge of disgust – but so too have artists like Goya. He is disturbingly honest – sometimes much to his own disadvantage.

Kerr wrote that the two had met through mutual friends when he was the federal minister for justice and he had begun collecting Adam's work. Occasionally, he stayed with Adam in the Blue Mountains. Adam painted him for the Archibald Prize, although the picture did not hang.

> I am aware that he, like many artists, has sometimes drunk too much, made bad choices and done silly things. I do not wish to diminish the seriousness of the charges he faces but these events perhaps fall into the latter category – unthinking, silly and wrong; but without any bad intentions ... I am confident you can deal with him as a person who is capable of flaws of judgment but not of underlying character.

*

It is decided the weapons offences will be dealt with under the *Mental Health (Forensic Provisions) Act*. Adam will have to accept a diagnosis and commit to a treatment plan. The guns will be destroyed. For the drink-driving charge, Adam will incur a ten-month suspended sentence. His licence will be taken away for five years. Adam is familiar with this. The magistrate has already read out his previous drink-driving offences: in 1997, 2003, 2004, 2006, 2007.

"Mr Cullen, you are a very intelligent man," she says. "You are a very artistic man – that is without doubt." She tells Adam he will need to develop "mental hardness" to deal with the issues that bedevil him. "There are some issues medically that are very serious and are beyond your help – they just happen. But if you can't curb your drinking, what you have to do is not be behind the wheel of a motor vehicle. If you wish to continue drinking – and it's not doing you any good – that is your decision. I do not believe at this point in time placing you in a custodial setting would be of any benefit to yourself or the community."

Kevin breaks down. It is reported next morning that he "dissolved in tears as his son was sentenced". Adam is silent. The magistrate asks if she has been clear.

"It's all extremely clear," Adam says. "Thank you, Your Honour."

She smiles at this apparently wild man: at his uncomfortable desire to address her correctly, at the schoolboy earnestness that matches his schoolboy crimes. "No. That's quite alright," she says. "I wish you well in your further endeavours, particularly your health."

Adam is quiet. Perhaps he is in shock. After four months of not knowing, he is free. He speaks briefly to the press outside. "It has certainly been a very trying episode," he says. "And I'm glad to be over it." There are a few more questions. Will he show again? Does he feel vindicated? He answers them without humour.

As one of the television reporters moves to leave, to pile into the overstuffed lifts of the Downing Centre, he catches her attention. "So, when is this going to be on?"

*

Adam is angry, angrier than I have ever seen him. A month has passed since he was sentenced and the resentment has built up inside him. He simmers with it.

"I'm really fucking bitter," he says. "You know what really pissed me off? It was the strip-search. Two fat fucking lesbians putting a torch under my balls and up my arse and taking photos of every fucking scar and tattoo. Nineteen photos of every fucking bit of my naked body. And I cried – not because of that, but for my dad. I cried there and I cried in my cell. It was that strip-search that broke me. That was like timber boards over my back. It just broke me."

The ignominy of it burns still, the sudden imposition of reality on a life lived by its own terms. "In the morning they threw me a paper bag with a sausage and egg McMuffin, cold coffee and warm orange juice. The orange juice was warmer than the coffee. The screw knew who I was. He baited me. He asked what scared me most about going to prison."

*

The psychiatric report prepared for Adam's defence is eviscerating to read. Its six pages are a vivid account of his life, rendered in the language of a humourless profession. Adam had seen the treating psychiatrist a few times in the 1990s, when his depression became obvious to all who knew him. He had tried prescribed medication but never committed to it. The drugs made him feel flat. A decade later, he submitted again to assessment.

Alcohol is the focus of the report and the expression of his illness. Addiction to drink was his inheritance, the psychiatrist found: a tendency for which he could blame a line of heavy-drinking relatives. Drunkenness was a means of tempering life. His mother's death, relationship breakdowns and the pressure of exhibiting had caused him to "crack", the report said.

> When asked about his alcohol intake, Mr Cullen said, 'I realise I have an alcohol problem ... I sort of have under control ... I was on a bottle per day for years ... now I only binge when I am working long hours or feel excited.'

Adam described intense anxiety: his heart raced before meetings, and he would sweat and be short of breath in anticipation of social occasions. He would feel physical tension throughout his body, and drink heavily before seeing people to alleviate these symptoms.

> Mr Cullen said that in retrospect he believes he had some periods of severe depression, which he said had never been successfully treated ... He reported periods of avoidance of company, negative thinking, anxiety symptoms, poor sleep patterns and self-doubt and self-recrimination. He said that he had dealt with low mood and anxiety by drinking heavily. He said, 'I like to work alone ... but it's so lonely ... I have to recall things ... I've entered this fluid economy where I just have to drink.'

Adam denied a number of things: that he had been referred for psychiatric treatment as a child, that he smoked cigarettes, that he was continuing to abuse opiates. The report noted that he arrived "eccentrically dressed" and smelling strongly of alcohol. His expressions were deemed "allusive, consistent with his upbringing in an artistic family and an underlying bipolar disorder". His intelligence was likely in the superior range, based on his vocabulary and reasoning. His hoarding of guns was regarded as consistent with "other professional artists who view a range of everyday objects as material for artistic expression and live their lives in a state of chaos and clutter that would be intolerable to other people".

The report found a "combination of disorders" that fell under Section 32 of the *Mental Health (Forensic Provisions) Act*. It recommended Adam commit to abstaining from alcohol, be admitted to a long-term residential alcohol rehabilitation program, and seek treatment for bipolar disorder.

> The diagnosis of alcohol dependence and abuse disorder is made on the basis of Mr Cullen's account of a pattern of regular hazardous drinking, and the reported pattern of his drinking and the complications of alcohol abuse, which include pancreatitis, amnestic episodes and a number of drink driving charges .
>
> The diagnosis of probable bipolar mood disorder is made on the basis of the history of a number of episodes of depression and episodes of sustained elevated mood accompanied by behaviour consistent with hypomania, including decreased need for

sleep, increased energy and creativity, and increased spending and sociability.

*

Adam is hollowed out by his final court appearance. It marks a turn in his mood that never corrects. "I'm so used to absolute freedom. I can shit anywhere. I can piss anywhere. I can take drugs. I can kill things. But in there I was nothing," he says. "For the first time in my life I felt what Ned Kelly felt. The last month has been hell. I don't think I was that mad. My own illness is news to me. They say that I'm borderline bipolar. That was odd – not to have the diagnosis but to swallow the diagnosis."

The treatment enforced on Adam by the court means he is seeing a psychiatrist each month. He can no longer ignore an illness that, in retrospect, has defined his life. "He's actually a really, really sweet man, but I just don't think he knows me very well. I lay down on a couch. He asks what I feel. And of course the arsehole makes me burst into tears about stuff I don't even think about."

Reality has had a strange impact on Adam. The stuff he doesn't think about is his life. He made excuses for his drinking, and when they gained no purchase he used his drinking as an excuse. "I have been making great art and I'm so happy, but I come out of the studio and I crash. I come home alone and I sleep alone and I crash."

He collapses into tears. "It's so embarrassing," he says. "Since court, a lot's changed. How I think – I suppose I'm learning to be a bit more responsible, which I don't think I should. I don't think anyone should have to live like we do. I think that's why I am alone. I have been persecuted. I was expecting jail. After that fucking search, I don't think I have cried that much since I was a teenager. Adam Cullen doesn't cry. But I met my match: I fought the law and they fucking won."

END

"The only thing the dead know is it's better to be alive."

The news was broken by the *Sydney Morning Herald*, just before six pm on 28 July 2012. Already it had the drab respectability of a wire story:

> The Archibald Prize-winning artist Adam Cullen, one of Australia's most collectable contemporary artists and well known for his distinctive portraits of high-profile Australians such as actor David Wenham, has died.
>
> The 46-year-old artist's lawyer and friend, Charles Waterstreet, confirmed Cullen's death to Fairfax Media.
>
> "I have just spoken to Adam's father Kevin [Cullen] who was with him yesterday," said Mr Waterstreet. Mr Waterstreet said Cullen had died in his sleep and was found by a family member today.
>
> "We have lost a great artist who lived and breathed the life of an artist," said Mr Waterstreet.
>
> Cullen, who lived on his own in Wentworth Falls, had been seriously ill for some time.

Soon it led the websites of the *Herald* and the *Australian.* It was on page three of both papers the following morning. The *Australian Financial Review* described his death as the "silent departure of an energised but disorderly artist". The Australian Associated Press ran several long filings on his career and his legacy. Were his mother alive to keep cuttings, she could have filled one of her folders in the course of the week that followed.

An obituary published in the *Australian* reported for the first time Adam's addiction to OxyContin. His years of alcoholism were covered, with one unnamed friend saying they had never seen Adam paint without first drinking an entire bottle of vodka.

"He had a gorgeous family and a beautiful upbringing as a grommet on the Northern Beaches," his last girlfriend, Cash Brown, said in the piece. "I just don't understand why he was so angry."

*

By the time I met Adam, he was hopelessly alone. He asked me to write this book – even invented for it a publishing contract – because he wanted me to be his friend. Eventually, he thought that friendship was love. He was isolated, his talent waning, his years of self-medication beginning at last to kill him. He had found in drugs his fatal cure. They had eaten away at him until there was nothing left.

In the end, I found him difficult to be around. I moved cities but still got daily phone calls. I stopped answering them. His demands were sad and unreasonable. He wanted more from me – to live together, that we travel together, that I quit my job and work for him. We would buy a house, he announced in one call, and I would write this book in its front room.

I did not expect to be so upset when I heard he had died. It was inevitable from the day we met, yet I was surprised by it. I was rattled by how the news affected me, by how grieved it made me. I drew a long bath and poured a scotch and I cried. They were despairing tears, as helpless as they were angry.

*

Adam did not suffer a formative tragedy. His childhood was a happy one. He wished it had not been. He spent his life rebelling against an upbringing less complicated than he had hoped it would be, less interesting. And yet he never really wanted to outgrow this childhood. He never wanted to become an adult.

Talent did odd things to Adam. It made him boastful, but at the same time wracked him with insecurity. He was incredibly controlling, and talent was the thing he could least control. His career reached exceptional heights, work that was occasionally sublime, but he seemed intent on ending it in wreckage. Eventually, this was the only course on which he could depend. He had become the broken men of his paintings. His observations of society's fringe, of the human car crashes he revelled in, had become a morose kind of self-portraiture. The whole time we knew each other, he had been alive at his own Irish wake.

I thought again of the Martin Bryant quote with which he chose to end his master's thesis. It was a prank, a provocation to those marking it. But it had something of the hopefulness I liked about Adam, his naive belief that if a few things had gone otherwise, the world would have been a different place. Perhaps, even, he might have been happy. I also hear Adam's blame, his contempt for responsibility: "I wanted to meet up with normal people but it didn't work."

*

The last time I saw Adam apparently happy, he was making plans in a notepad to leave Wentworth Falls and buy a farm in Rylstone. He drew pictures of the homestead, childish blueprints for the life he fantasised about living. "I'll get some horses. Two horses, some dogs, maybe some cattle," he said. "Put them on the bottle. Have a caretaker to look after them, clean the house, mow the lawn. It sounds like heaven. That's where I'd die. I could do a lot of damage and leave a lot of aesthetic residue."

Adam brought up suicide again. "I've never been one for suicide. That's such a cop-out," he said. "I can't understand anyone who wants to blow their brains out. Stay alive, it's good. The only thing the dead know is it's better to be alive."

The final line, gently paraphrased, belonged to the Stanley Kubrick film *Full Metal Jacket.* So much of Adam was paraphrased, I saw as I went through my notepads. Alongside his draughtsmanship, it was his most reliable technique. He was an assemblage. He was always pilfering – "transcribing", as he put it. The line with which he buried his mother was Jim Morrison's, as were the kicks he was getting before the treehouse went up in flames. His diary entries were an homage to Camus: "Mother died today. Or maybe yesterday, I don't know."

*

Adam left hospital for the final time in a taxi, stopping off to buy a bottle of vodka en route to his studio. A week earlier he had been in a coma; a month later, he would be dead. His liver was failing, his stomach the source of undiagnosed complications.

Before the coma, nurses and social workers had begun refusing to enter his house. The squalor had become too much. While he lay in hospital, his family had sent in the cleaners. The carpets were pulled up. His mattress, which had putrefied, was thrown out. Having discharged himself from the ward, Adam slept that first night on his bearskin. The next day, he disappeared.

When Adam's cousin tracked him down, he was being thrown out of the Rest Easy Motel on the edge of the Great Western Highway. A manager had found him in the room, covered in vomit, and refused to continue his accommodation.

It was by taxi that Adam arrived at his schoolfriend Jason Martin's house in Sydney, with handfuls of cash and bags of cheese and ham. He was so weak he could scarcely move, sleeping most of the day and watching hours of television. He stayed for more than a week, with two buckets beside the bed – one for vomit, one for piss. He fixated on food. In the middle of the night he would wake and demand bacon. He would order elaborate pizzas, then not eat them. The final drawings he made were of screaming heads and sausages and a bowl of something he had labelled salad.

"A doctor came to look at him," Jason told me. "He said, 'I would get this guy straight to emergency at Prince Alfred.' Adam just refused to go. The doctor said, 'It's good. You're doing your best. But you're just postponing the inevitable.'"

Adam made it home briefly. He believed that if he returned to his own bed, he would be well again. He wasn't. When his cousin found him for the last time, he was curled on a mattress, facing the only window in the room. Varicose veins in his oesophagus had ruptured, a complication of liver failure. He drowned in his own blood.

ACKNOWLEDGEMENTS

My first thanks are to Adam, for everything. And then to the other people who spoke to me for this book, who filled in everything else. Thanks especially to the executors of Adam's estate: Kevin Cullen and Jason Martin.

On a personal note, I thank David Marr. He was the first person I spoke to about writing this biography, and his sensible advice is woven through it.

Thank you to Margaret Fink for the courage I borrowed and the lines I stole. And to TV Moore, my adoptive brother, who told me not to write a dainty book. I hope I have managed.

Thank you to Tamara Dean for the photograph that became this book's original cover, and to Helen Garner and Christos Tsiolkas for the kind words they put on it. Thanks also to Dale Frank for the conversation that became its prologue.

I have leant on the advice of a lot of people for this book – Kate Jennings, Brigid Delaney, Nick Feik, Josephine Tovey, Alice Gage, Nick O'Malley, Edie Atkins – and all have been invaluable. My family has been good, too. I wouldn't be a writer without them.

Thank you to Chris Feik for believing this might be a book and, with Julian Welch, editing it to become one. And to Siân Scott-Clash for keeping it on track.

And, of course, Morry Schwartz: my boss, friend, and now publisher. I am endlessly grateful for his enthusiasm and envious of his energy.

Finally, to Penny Schofield, who taught shorthand to me and another two generations of journalists. Your lessons are on every page.

ERIK JENSEN is the founding editor of *The Saturday Paper*. He has written for film, television and the stage, and worked as a writer and editor at *The Sydney Morning Herald*, where he won the Walkley Award for Young Print Journalist of the Year and the United Nations Association of Australia Media Peace Prize. *Acute Misfortune* won the Nib Award for Literature and was shortlisted for the Walkley Book Award and the Victorian Premier's Literary Awards. His second book is *On Kate Jennings*.